Ultimate Study Guide for FTCE Professional Education Test (083)

Teacher Certification Prep Introduction

Michelle Mann

Introduction

Welcome to The Ultimate Study Guide for FTCE Professional Education Test: Teacher Certification Prep. In this introduction, we'll explain the comprehensive landscape of the Florida Teacher Certification Examinations (FTCE) Professional Education Test.

This test is designed to assess the proficiency and readiness of aspiring educators in the state of Florida. The FTCE Professional Education Test serves as a pivotal milestone in your journey toward becoming a certified educator in the state.

Overview of the FTCE Professional Education Test

The FTCE Professional Education Test serves as a pivotal checkpoint within the intricate certification process tailored for educators in the vibrant educational landscape of Florida. More than just a mere assessment, it stands as a sentinel guarding the gates to the esteemed profession of teaching,

Introduction

evaluating candidates not merely on their grasp of theoretical concepts but on their ability to translate that knowledge into effective pedagogical practices. It is a meticulous evaluation that delves deep into the heart of educational principles, scrutinizing candidates' acumen in areas ranging from curriculum development and instructional strategies to classroom management and ethical conduct.

In essence, the FTCE Professional Education Test is a testament to Florida's commitment to fostering a cadre of educators who are not only well-versed in subject matter content but are also equipped with the essential tools and competencies needed to navigate the dynamic and multifaceted environment of the modern classroom. It serves as a beacon guiding aspiring educators toward the shores of proficiency and excellence, ensuring that they possess the requisite skills and insights to inspire, educate, and empower future generations of Floridians.

Through its comprehensive evaluation, the FTCE Professional Education Test not only assesses candidates' theoretical knowledge but also challenges them to demonstrate their practical application of pedagogical theories within diverse educational settings. It endeavors to cultivate educators who are not merely repositories of information but dynamic facilitators of learning, capable of adapting to the unique needs and challenges of their students while upholding the highest standards of professionalism and ethical conduct.

In summary, the FTCE Professional Education Test stands as a hallmark of Florida's dedication to fostering a community of educators who are not only academically proficient but are also compassionate, innovative, and dedicated to the noble cause of education. It is a rite of passage that signifies the transition from a student of education to a

Introduction

steward of knowledge, marking the beginning of a journey filled with opportunities to inspire, shape, and transform the lives of countless individuals through the power of education.

Why is this Test Important for Florida Educators?

The significance of the FTCE Professional Education Test for aspiring educators in Florida cannot be overstated. It stands as a formidable gatekeeper, regulating entry into the esteemed fraternity of educators while simultaneously symbolizing a commitment to the noble ideals of excellence and professionalism in education.

At its core, the FTCE Professional Education Test serves as a rigorous evaluation of a candidate's readiness to assume the mantle of an educator. It not only gauges their proficiency in educational theory and pedagogical practices but also assesses their dedication to upholding the highest standards of teaching excellence. By successfully navigating this formidable assessment, candidates demonstrate not only their academic prowess but also their unwavering dedication to the vocation of teaching.

Moreover, the FTCE Professional Education Test serves as a litmus test for the foundational competencies that underpin effective teaching. It evaluates candidates on their ability to engage students, design instructional strategies tailored to diverse learning styles, and create inclusive and supportive classroom environments conducive to learning and growth. In essence, it seeks to ensure that aspiring educators possess the essential skills and dispositions necessary to foster the intellectual, social, and emotional development of their students.

Introduction

Beyond being a mere prerequisite for certification, the successful completion of the FTCE Professional Education Test is emblematic of a candidate's commitment to lifelong learning and professional growth. It signifies their willingness to invest in their development as educators, continuously honing their craft and staying abreast of emerging trends and best practices in the field of education. In this way, passing the FTCE Professional Education Test marks not just the beginning but a continual journey toward excellence in teaching.

The FTCE Professional Education Test serves as a cornerstone of Florida's educational landscape, ensuring that only the most qualified and dedicated individuals are entrusted with the responsibility of shaping the minds of future generations. It is a testament to the state's unwavering commitment to fostering a culture of educational excellence and innovation, one teacher at a time.

Structure and Format of the Test

The structure and format of the FTCE Professional Education Test are meticulously crafted to encapsulate the breadth and depth of pedagogical knowledge essential for effective teaching. It is a multifaceted examination designed to probe not only the theoretical underpinnings of education but also the practical application of these principles in the dynamic landscape of the classroom.

At its core, the test is structured to encompass a diverse array of topics and competencies relevant to the field of education. From theories of learning and human development to instructional strategies and assessment techniques, the FTCE Professional Education Test leaves no stone unturned in its quest to assess candidates' readiness to step

Introduction

into the role of an educator. Each question is carefully crafted to gauge not only the depth of candidates' understanding but also their ability to synthesize and apply knowledge in real-world teaching scenarios.

Central to the format of the FTCE Professional Education Test are multiple-choice questions, chosen for their efficacy in assessing a wide range of content areas in a standardized and objective manner. These questions are meticulously curated to cover the spectrum of educational domains, from curriculum design and classroom management to educational law and ethics. Candidates are challenged to navigate through a series of thought-provoking scenarios, each requiring careful analysis and reasoned judgment to arrive at the correct answer.

Moreover, the test is structured to reflect the complexities and nuances of the teaching profession, with questions often presented in the context of authentic classroom scenarios. This format not only tests candidates' theoretical knowledge but also their ability to apply that knowledge in practical, real-world settings. From addressing the diverse needs of students to navigating the intricacies of educational policy, the FTCE Professional Education Test challenges candidates to demonstrate their competence and expertise across a spectrum of professional practices.

In essence, the structure and format of the FTCE Professional Education Test are a testament to the rigorous standards upheld by the state of Florida in its quest to ensure the highest quality of education for its students. It is a comprehensive examination that reflects the multifaceted nature of the teaching profession, serving as a benchmark against which aspiring educators' knowledge, skills, and abilities are measured. Through its carefully crafted questions and scenarios, the test not only evaluates candidates'

Introduction

readiness for certification but also prepares them for the challenges and rewards that await them in the noble vocation of teaching.

Scoring and Passing Criteria

Scoring and passing criteria on the FTCE Professional Education Test are intricately woven into the fabric of educational standards, serving as a beacon of proficiency and excellence for aspiring educators navigating the certification process in Florida. A meticulous blend of precision and rigor, the scoring system ensures that candidates are thoroughly evaluated on their mastery of pedagogical principles and their ability to translate theoretical knowledge into practical classroom application.

Central to the scoring mechanism is the tallying of correctly answered questions, each serving as a testament to a candidate's depth of understanding and aptitude in the field of education. With each accurate response, candidates inch closer to the coveted threshold of proficiency, their scores serving as a barometer of their readiness to embark on the journey of teaching with confidence and competence.

However, beyond mere numerical tallies, the passing criteria set forth by the Florida Department of Education serve as a beacon guiding candidates toward the pinnacle of success. This minimum score, meticulously determined through rigorous evaluation and expert calibration, represents the gold standard of knowledge and competency expected from certified educators in the state. It is a benchmark that underscores the importance of maintaining the highest standards of excellence in the noble profession of teaching, ensuring that only the most qualified individuals

Introduction

are entrusted with the responsibility of shaping the minds of future generations.

Achieving this minimum score is not merely a milestone; it is a testament to a candidate's dedication, perseverance, and unwavering commitment to the principles of education. It signifies more than just proficiency; it represents a mastery of the core competencies essential for effective teaching and learning. By surpassing this threshold, candidates demonstrate their readiness to step into the classroom with confidence, equipped with the knowledge, skills, and abilities necessary to inspire, motivate, and empower their students to reach their fullest potential.

In essence, the scoring and passing criteria of the FTCE Professional Education Test serve as a cornerstone of Florida's educational landscape, ensuring that only the most qualified and competent individuals are granted the privilege of becoming certified educators. It is a testament to the state's unwavering commitment to excellence in education, underscoring the importance of maintaining the highest standards of proficiency and professionalism in the noble vocation of teaching.

Understanding the Test Content

Understanding the depth and breadth of the content covered in the FTCE Professional Education Test is paramount for aspiring educators as they prepare to embark on their journey toward certification. The test serves as a comprehensive assessment of essential knowledge and competencies that are fundamental to effective teaching and learning practices in Florida's educational landscape.

Spanning across a diverse array of topics, the content of the FTCE Professional Education Test encompasses the

Introduction

rich tapestry of educational theory and practice. From the intricate workings of educational psychology, where candidates explore the intricacies of human cognition and motivation, to the dynamic realm of instructional strategies, where innovative pedagogical approaches are explored to engage and inspire diverse learners.

Moreover, candidates must demonstrate proficiency in assessment techniques, understanding the nuances of formative and summative assessment practices, as well as the ability to analyze and interpret assessment data to inform instructional decision-making. Additionally, a firm grasp of professional ethics and standards of conduct is essential, as educators are entrusted with the profound responsibility of nurturing the minds and hearts of future generations.

In the pages that follow, this book endeavors to unravel the complexities of each facet of the FTCE Professional Education Test, offering invaluable insights, strategies, and resources to help candidates navigate the vast expanse of test content with confidence and competence. Through comprehensive explanations, illustrative examples, and practical tips, readers will gain a deeper understanding of key concepts and acquire the tools and strategies necessary to excel in the examination.

Whether you are embarking on your journey towards certification as a novice educator or seeking to enhance your pedagogical prowess as a seasoned professional, this book serves as your trusted companion and guide. With its holistic approach to test preparation, it aims to empower educators at every stage of their career journey, equipping them with the knowledge, skills, and confidence needed to succeed in the FTCE Professional Education Test and beyond.

Introduction

So, as you immerse yourself in the pages that lie ahead, remember that you are not merely preparing for an examination; you are embarking on a transformative journey towards becoming a proficient and impactful educator, poised to make a meaningful difference in the lives of countless students across the Sunshine State.

Chapter 1
Detailed Breakdown of Test Domains

Within the expansive realm of the FTCE Professional Education Test lie distinct domains, each a microcosm of essential knowledge and skills vital for aspiring educators. We'll delve into these domains, unraveling their intricacies and shedding light on the key competencies they assess.

6 Test Domains

The FTCE Professional Education Test covers 6 domains:

Foundational Knowledge

Foundational Knowledge is a crucial domain in the FTCE Professional Education Test, assessing candidates' understanding of key educational theories, principles, and philosophies. Topics include theories of learning, educational psychology, and historical and philosophical foundations of education. Candidates delve into diverse perspectives, from behaviorism to constructivism, and explore human cognition, motivation, and development. They also trace the evolution of educational thought throughout history. Mastery of this domain equips candidates with a solid foundation for effective teaching and learning practices.

Student Development & Learning

In the Student Development and Learning domain of the FTCE Professional Education Test, candidates demonstrate their understanding of human development theories and their application to student learning. Topics include cognitive, social, emotional, and physical development, as well as learning theories and factors influencing learning. Candidates explore the complexities of human growth and maturation, apply developmental theories to educational practices, and examine various factors that impact student learning. Mastery of this domain equips candidates to create learning environments that promote holistic student development and academic success.

Assessment & Evaluation

The Assessment and Evaluation domain of the FTCE Professional Education Test focuses on candidates' understanding of assessment principles, techniques, and practices. Topics include formative and summative assessment, standardized testing, assessment data analysis, and using assessment data to inform instructional decision-making. Candidates explore various assessment methods, learn to interpret assessment results, and understand how to use assessment data effectively in planning and adjusting instruction to meet student needs. Mastery of this domain equips candidates with essential skills in assessment literacy, enabling them to contribute effectively to student learning and success.

Instructional Design & Planning

The Instructional Design and Planning domain of the

FTCE Professional Education Test evaluates candidates' ability to design and implement effective instruction. Topics include instructional design models, curriculum development, lesson planning, differentiation, and instructional strategies for diverse learners. Candidates learn to create cohesive lesson plans aligned with learning objectives, accommodate diverse learner needs, and employ various instructional strategies. Mastery of this domain equips candidates with the skills to design engaging and effective learning experiences for all students.

Learning Environment & Classroom Management

The Learning Environment and Classroom Management domain of the FTCE Professional Education Test evaluates candidates on their knowledge and application of strategies for creating positive learning environments and managing classroom behavior. Topics include classroom management theories, strategies for promoting positive behavior, and addressing challenging behaviors. Candidates learn to establish clear expectations, build positive relationships, and implement proactive measures to create supportive learning environments. Mastery of this domain equips candidates with skills to foster a conducive atmosphere for student growth and success.

Professional Responsibility & Ethical Conduct

The Professional Responsibility and Ethical Conduct domain of the FTCE Professional Education Test evaluates candidates on their comprehension of professional ethics, legal obligations, and ethical behavior in teaching. Topics include understanding professional codes of conduct, legal requirements for educators, and ethical decision-making.

Candidates learn to uphold integrity, navigate legal frameworks, and make ethical decisions in their professional practice. Mastery of this domain ensures educators are equipped to maintain high ethical standards and contribute positively to the educational community.

Key Competencies and Skills Assessed

The key competencies and skills assessed by the FTCE Professional Education Test include:

- Pedagogical Knowledge: Candidates are evaluated on their understanding of educational theories, principles, and practices, including instructional design, assessment, and classroom management.
- Student Development and Learning: Candidates demonstrate knowledge of human development theories and their ability to apply this knowledge to promote student learning and development across cognitive, social, emotional, and physical domains.
- Assessment and Evaluation: Candidates showcase their proficiency in assessment principles, techniques, and practices, including formative and summative assessment, standardized testing, and data analysis to inform instructional decision-making.
- Instructional Design and Planning: Candidates exhibit their ability to design and implement effective instruction, incorporating instructional design models, curriculum development, lesson planning, differentiation,

and instructional strategies for diverse learners.
- Learning Environment and Classroom Management: Candidates demonstrate strategies for creating positive learning environments and managing classroom behavior, including classroom management theories, promoting positive behavior, and addressing challenging behaviors.
- Professional Responsibility and Ethical Conduct: Candidates showcase their understanding of professional ethics, legal responsibilities, and ethical decision-making in the teaching profession, including adherence to professional codes of conduct and compliance with legal requirements for educators.

These competencies and skills collectively assess candidates' readiness to excel as educators in the state of Florida, ensuring they possess the knowledge and abilities necessary for effective teaching and promoting student success.

Overview of Topics Covered

The FTCE Professional Education Test encompasses a comprehensive overview of essential topics that are fundamental to the field of education. Let's delve deeper into each area covered:

Educational Theories and Philosophies

Candidates explore the rich tapestry of educational theories and philosophies that underpin the practice of teaching. This includes studying prominent theorists such as John Dewey, Lev Vygotsky, and Jean Piaget, and understanding their contributions to pedagogical thought. Additionally, candidates analyze various educational philosophies, from perennialism to progressivism, and consider how these philosophies inform instructional practices and approaches to curriculum design.

Human Development Theories

Understanding the developmental journey of learners is crucial for effective teaching. Candidates delve into human development theories, examining stages of cognitive, social, emotional, and physical growth from infancy through adulthood. This knowledge allows educators to tailor their instruction to meet the diverse needs and developmental stages of their students.

Assessment Principles and Techniques

Assessment is a cornerstone of effective teaching and learning. Candidates learn about assessment principles and techniques, including formative and summative assessment, authentic assessment, and performance-based assessment. They explore strategies for designing assessments aligned with learning objectives, interpreting assessment data, and using assessment results to inform instructional decision-making.

Instructional Design Models and Strategies

Instructional design is the process of creating engaging and effective learning experiences for students. Candidates study various instructional design models, such as the ADDIE model and the TPACK framework, and explore strategies for designing instruction that is engaging, accessible, and aligned with learning goals. They also learn about different instructional strategies, such as direct instruction, inquiry-based learning, and cooperative learning, and consider how to integrate technology effectively into instruction.

Classroom Management Theories and Strategies

Effective classroom management is essential for creating a positive and productive learning environment. Candidates explore theories of classroom management, such as behaviorism and constructivism, and learn strategies for establishing clear expectations, promoting positive behavior, and addressing challenging behaviors. They also consider the role of teacher-student relationships, classroom organization, and culturally responsive practices in fostering a supportive learning environment.

Professional Ethics and Legal Responsibilities

Educators are held to high ethical and professional standards. Candidates examine professional codes of conduct and ethical guidelines for educators, including principles of integrity, fairness, and professionalism. They also learn about legal responsibilities related to student confidentiality, special education laws, and mandated reporting requirements. Understanding these ethical and legal considerations ensures that educators uphold the trust and integrity of the teaching profession while providing a safe and inclusive learning environment for all students.

In summary, the FTCE Professional Education Test covers a breadth of topics essential for aspiring educators, equipping them with the knowledge and skills needed to excel in the dynamic and challenging field of education.

Chapter 2
Test-Taking Strategies

In the journey towards achieving success in the FTCE Professional Education Test, mastering effective test-taking strategies is crucial. This chapter serves as a comprehensive guide, offering valuable insights and practical tips to help candidates navigate the examination with confidence and poise.

Effective Techniques to Study for the FTCE Professional Education Test

In the pursuit of excellence on the FTCE Professional Education Test, establishing effective study techniques forms the cornerstone of preparation. This section delves into the strategies and methodologies that lay the groundwork for comprehensive understanding and retention of key concepts.

Create a Structured Study Schedule

Begin by crafting a study schedule that provides a roadmap for your preparation journey. Allocate dedicated time slots for reviewing different content areas and topics covered in the test. Ensure a balance between subjects, giving more focus to areas where you may need additional reinforcement. Setting specific goals and deadlines can help you stay accountable and on track.

Utilize Diverse Study Resources

Variety is key when it comes to study resources. Expand your arsenal by incorporating a mix of textbooks, online materials, practice tests, and flashcards. Textbooks offer in-depth explanations and examples, while online resources provide interactive learning experiences and supplemental materials. Practice tests simulate the exam environment and help gauge your progress, while flashcards are excellent for quick review of key concepts.

Engage in Active Learning

Passive reading alone may not suffice for effective comprehension and retention. Engage in active learning strategies that encourage deeper understanding and critical thinking. Summarize content in your own words, create study guides or concept maps to organize information visually, and teach concepts to others—whether it's a friend, family member, or even a pet. Teaching reinforces your understanding and highlights areas where further clarification may be needed.

Take Regular Breaks and Prioritize Self-Care

Studying for extended periods without breaks can lead to burnout and diminished productivity. Incorporate regular breaks into your study sessions to rest and recharge your mind. Use breaks to engage in activities that promote relaxation and well-being, such as going for a walk, practicing mindfulness or meditation, or indulging in a hobby you enjoy. Prioritize self-care by getting adequate sleep, staying hydrated, and nourishing your body with nutritious meals.

Review and Adapt

As you progress in your study journey, regularly assess your understanding and identify areas of strength and weakness. Review your study schedule and adjust it as needed to allocate more time to challenging topics or content areas. Be flexible and open to modifying your study strategies based on what works best for you. Don't hesitate to seek help from tutors, study groups, or online forums if you encounter difficulties or have questions.

By incorporating these effective study techniques into your preparation routine, you lay a solid foundation for success on the FTCE Professional Education Test. Remember, consistency, dedication, and a strategic approach are key as you embark on this journey towards achieving your goals.

Tips for Effective Time Management when Studying

In the high-stakes environment of the FTCE Professional Education Test, effective time management is not just advantageous—it's imperative. This section outlines actionable strategies to optimize your use of time during both study sessions and the actual exam.

Practice Pacing During Study Sessions

Start by familiarizing yourself with the time constraints of the test. During study sessions and practice tests, simulate the time limits imposed by the actual exam. This allows you to gauge how much time you can allocate to each question or section. Aim to strike a balance between thoroughness and efficiency, ensuring that you cover all relevant material without sacrificing accuracy.

Prioritize Questions Based on Difficulty

Not all questions carry equal weight in terms of difficulty or point value. Prioritize your approach by tackling easier questions first to build momentum and confidence. Reserve more time for challenging questions that may require deeper analysis or critical thinking. This strategic allocation of time ensures that you maximize your potential for earning points while minimizing the risk of getting bogged down by complex questions.

Use Marking for Review Wisely

If you encounter a particularly challenging question, resist the temptation to dwell on it indefinitely. Instead, mark it for review and move on to the next question. This prevents you from getting stuck in a time-consuming cycle of indecision. By marking questions for review, you create a strategic reserve of time to revisit them later, allowing you to approach them with fresh perspective or utilize leftover time at the end of the exam.

Answer All Questions Within Allotted Time

One of the cardinal rules of time management in exams is to answer all questions within the allotted time. Avoid leaving any questions unanswered, as unanswered questions automatically result in missed opportunities for earning points. If time is running short, make educated guesses rather than leaving questions blank. Remember, there is no penalty for incorrect answers, so take advantage of every opportunity to earn points.

Allocate Time for Review and Revisions

As you near the end of the exam, reserve a few minutes to review your work and make any necessary revisions. Use this time to double-check your answers, ensuring accuracy and completeness. Look out for any questions you may have skipped or marked for review earlier and allocate time to revisit them. Trust your instincts and avoid making unnecessary changes unless you're certain of an error.

By implementing these time management tips into your study routine and exam strategy, you can approach the FTCE Professional Education Test with confidence and efficiency. Remember, effective time management is not just about rushing through questions—it's about strategically allocating your time to maximize your potential for success.

Strategies for Multiple-Choice Questions

Multiple-choice questions constitute a significant portion of the FTCE Professional Education Test, demanding a strategic approach to ensure accuracy and efficiency. This section outlines a systematic methodology for tackling these questions with confidence and precision.

Careful Reading and Analysis

Begin by approaching each multiple-choice question with a focused and analytical mindset. Carefully read the question stem and all answer choices, ensuring a thorough understanding of the context and requirements. Pay attention to nuances in wording and identify any key terms or phrases that may provide clues to the correct answer.

Eliminate Obviously Incorrect Choices

Once you've grasped the essence of the question, systematically evaluate each answer choice. Begin by eliminating any choices that are clearly incorrect or irrelevant to the question stem. Look for discrepancies in logic, factual inaccuracies, or options that are inconsistent with the information provided.

Weigh Remaining Options

After eliminating obviously incorrect choices, shift your focus to the remaining options. Compare and contrast these options, considering their relevance to the question stem and their alignment with the content covered in your study materials. Evaluate each option based on its level of specificity, coherence, and logical consistency.

Identify Keywords and Phrases

Pay close attention to keywords and phrases within the question stem that may offer insights into the correct answer. Look for qualifiers such as "not," "except," or "most likely," as these can significantly alter the meaning of the question. Similarly, identify contextual clues or cues that may direct you towards the correct response.

Make Educated Guesses

In instances where you're unsure of the correct answer, don't hesitate to make an educated guess. Utilize the process of elimination to narrow down your options and increase the likelihood of selecting the correct response. Remember, there is no penalty for guessing on the FTCE Professional Education Test, so it's always advantageous to provide a response rather than leaving a question blank.

Maintain a Strategic Pace

While it's essential to approach each question methodically, it's equally important to maintain a strategic pace throughout the exam. Avoid spending too much time on any single question, as this can impede your progress and compromise your ability to complete the entire test within the allotted time. If you find yourself stuck on a particular question, mark it for review and move on to the next one.

By implementing these strategies for multiple-choice questions into your test-taking approach, you can navigate the complexities of the FTCE Professional Education Test with confidence and precision. Remember to remain focused, trust your instincts, and utilize your knowledge and analytical skills to select the most appropriate response for each question.

Dealing with Test Anxiety: Confidently Overcoming Challenges

For many candidates, confronting test anxiety is an inevitable hurdle on the path to success in the FTCE Professional Education Test. However, armed with effective strategies, you can navigate through this challenge and perform at your best. This section explores various techniques to manage test anxiety and cultivate a mindset of confidence and resilience.

Practice Relaxation Techniques

Before and during the test, employ relaxation techniques to calm your nerves and alleviate anxiety. Deep breathing exercises can help regulate your breathing and induce a sense of calmness. Visualize yourself succeeding in the exam, envisioning a positive outcome and feeling confident in your abilities. Alternatively, engage in progressive muscle relaxation by tensing and releasing different muscle groups to release tension and promote relaxation.

Maintain a Positive Mindset

Cultivate a positive mindset by focusing on your preparation efforts and past successes. Remind yourself of the hours you've dedicated to studying and the progress you've made along the way. Visualize yourself overcoming challenges and performing well on the test. Challenge negative thoughts or self-doubt by replacing them with affirmations of confidence and competence. Repeat positive affirmations such as "I am well-prepared and capable of succeeding" to reinforce your belief in yourself.

Implement Stress-Reducing Strategies

Incorporate stress-reducing strategies into your daily routine to mitigate anxiety leading up to the test. Practice self-care activities such as exercise, meditation, or spending time outdoors to promote relaxation and well-being. Get adequate sleep in the days leading up to the exam to ensure optimal cognitive function and alertness. Avoid excessive caffeine or stimulants on the day of the test, as they can exacerbate feelings of anxiety.

Utilize Positive Coping Mechanisms

Develop positive coping mechanisms to manage anxiety during the test itself. If you feel overwhelmed or anxious, take a moment to pause and practice deep breathing or mindfulness techniques to regain your composure. Focus on the present moment and tackle each question one at a time, rather than getting caught up in worrying about future questions or outcomes. Remind yourself that feeling nervous is normal and that you have the skills and knowledge necessary to succeed.

Seek Support

Don't hesitate to seek support from friends, family, or trusted mentors if you're struggling with test anxiety. Talking about your concerns with others can provide validation and reassurance, helping to alleviate feelings of stress and anxiety. Consider reaching out to a counselor or mental health professional for additional support and guidance in managing test-related anxiety.

By implementing these strategies for dealing with test anxiety, you can approach the FTCE Professional Education Test with confidence, resilience, and a positive mindset.

Remember that feeling nervous is a natural response to challenging situations, but with the right tools and techniques, you can overcome anxiety and perform at your best. Trust in your preparation and believe in your ability to succeed—you've got this!

Setting Yourself Up for Success: Tips for Test Day

As the day of the FTCE Professional Education Test dawns, strategic preparation and mindful practices can help you navigate the challenges ahead with confidence and composure. Here's a comprehensive guide to ensure you make the most of the test day:

Arrive Early and Prepared

Arriving early to the testing center allows ample time for check-in procedures and familiarizing yourself with the testing environment. Aim to arrive at least 30 minutes before the scheduled start time. Double-check that you have all required identification documents, such as a valid government-issued ID, your admission ticket, and any approved testing aids. Arriving early helps alleviate stress and ensures a smooth start to your testing experience.

Fuel Your Body and Mind

Start your day with a nutritious meal that provides sustained energy and mental clarity. Choose foods rich in complex carbohydrates, lean proteins, and healthy fats to fuel your brain and body for optimal performance. Avoid heavy or greasy meals that may cause discomfort or sluggishness during the exam. Stay hydrated by drinking water throughout the day to maintain alertness and prevent dehydration.

Maintain Focus and Minimize Distractions

Once seated for the exam, focus your attention solely on the task at hand. Minimize distractions by silencing your phone and avoiding unnecessary movements or conversations with other test-takers. Stay centered and composed, anchoring yourself in the present moment. If you find your mind wandering or feeling overwhelmed, take a few deep breaths to center yourself and regain focus.

Pace Yourself and Manage Time Wisely

Pacing yourself is crucial for success on the FTCE Professional Education Test. Allocate time strategically to each section, ensuring that you have sufficient time to answer all questions thoroughly. Monitor your progress throughout the exam and adjust your pace accordingly. If you encounter particularly challenging questions, don't dwell too long—mark them for review and move on to maximize your efficiency.

Take Breaks if Needed

Listen to your body and take short breaks if needed to rest and recharge. Use breaks to stretch, take a few deep breaths, or simply clear your mind before returning to the exam. Be mindful of the time allotted for breaks and ensure that you use them judiciously to maintain momentum without sacrificing valuable testing time.

Trust in Your Preparation and Abilities

Above all, trust in the preparation and hard work you've invested in preparing for the exam. Believe in your abilities and approach each question with confidence and determination. Remember that you've equipped yourself with the knowledge and skills necessary to succeed. Stay calm, stay focused, and trust in your ability to perform at your best.

By incorporating these tips into your test day routine,

you can approach the FTCE Professional Education Test with confidence, composure, and a strategic mindset. Stay grounded, stay resilient, and remember that success is within your reach. You've prepared diligently for this moment—now it's time to shine!

Chapter 3
In-Depth Review of Test Domains

The FTCE Professional Education Test evaluates candidates across five key domains, each essential for success in the field of education. This chapter provides an exhaustive exploration of each domain, offering insights into the core competencies and skills assessed within each domain.

Domain 1: Instructional Design and Planning

Learning Theories and Applications

In this domain, candidates embark on an exploration of foundational learning theories and their practical applications within educational contexts. They delve into prominent theories such as behaviorism, cognitivism, constructivism, and connectivism, each offering unique perspectives on how individuals acquire knowledge and skills. Candidates analyze the implications of these theories for instructional design and student learning outcomes, considering factors such as motivation, engagement, and retention. By understanding the underpinnings of various learning theories, candidates can make informed decisions when designing instruction and selecting appropriate teaching strategies to meet the diverse needs of learners.

Curriculum Development

This section immerses candidates in the principles and practices of curriculum development, a cornerstone of effective teaching and learning. Candidates learn to conceptualize, design, implement, and evaluate curriculum frameworks that align with educational standards and cater to the diverse needs of students. They explore curriculum models, such as the Tyler model and the Taba model, and consider factors such as scope, sequence, and alignment with learning objectives. Through hands-on experiences and case studies, candidates develop the skills and expertise necessary to create meaningful and engaging learning experiences that promote student success and achievement.

Assessment Strategies

Candidates in this domain acquire mastery in assessment principles, techniques, and practices essential for gauging student learning and informing instructional decision-making. They explore a variety of assessment strategies, including formative assessments that provide ongoing feedback to guide instruction and summative assessments that measure student achievement at the end of a unit or course. Candidates delve into authentic assessment methods that mirror real-world tasks and scenarios, allowing students to demonstrate their knowledge and skills in meaningful contexts. Moreover, candidates learn to analyze assessment data effectively, identify trends and patterns, and use data to adjust instruction and support student growth. By integrating assessment seamlessly into the instructional process, candidates ensure that learning experiences are purposeful, relevant, and aligned with learning objectives.

In summary, Domain 1 equips candidates with the knowledge and skills needed to design, plan, and implement effective instruction that fosters student learning and achievement. Through an in-depth exploration of learning theories, curriculum development principles, and assessment strategies, candidates are prepared to create dynamic and engaging learning experiences that meet the diverse needs of learners and promote educational excellence.

Domain 2: Learning Environment and Student Engagement

Classroom Management Techniques

Candidates in this domain delve into the art and science of classroom management, mastering strategies for creating and maintaining positive and inclusive learning environments. Drawing from classroom management theories and research, candidates explore effective behavior management strategies, proactive approaches to discipline, and techniques for establishing clear expectations and routines. They learn to cultivate a climate of respect, responsibility, and mutual trust, where students feel safe, supported, and motivated to engage in learning. Through hands-on experiences and simulations, candidates develop the skills and confidence necessary to navigate diverse classroom dynamics and effectively manage student behavior while maximizing instructional time.

Motivation and Communication Strategies

This section focuses on the critical role of motivation and communication in fostering student engagement and academic success. Candidates explore motivational theories and techniques aimed at inspiring and empowering learners to set and achieve meaningful goals. They develop proficiency in communication strategies tailored to diverse learners, including active listening, effective questioning techniques, and empathetic communication. Candidates also learn to leverage technology and multimedia tools to enhance communication and facilitate collaboration among students. By fostering open and inclusive communication channels, candidates create an environment where students feel valued, heard, and motivated to participate actively in their own learning journey.

Diversity and Inclusion in the Classroom

Candidates in this domain examine the principles of diversity, equity, and inclusion and their implications for teaching and learning. They explore strategies for creating culturally responsive learning environments that honor and celebrate students' diverse backgrounds, experiences, and perspectives. Candidates learn to address the needs of diverse student populations, including English language learners, students with disabilities, and students from marginalized or underrepresented groups. They develop sensitivity to issues of social justice and equity in education and explore ways to promote inclusive practices that affirm and empower all learners. By embracing diversity and fostering a culture of respect and acceptance, candidates create classrooms where every student feels valued, supported, and capable of achieving their full potential.

In summary, Domain 2 equips candidates with the knowledge, skills, and dispositions necessary to create inclusive, engaging, and supportive learning environments that promote student success and well-being. Through mastery of classroom management techniques, motivation and communication strategies, and principles of diversity and inclusion, candidates cultivate classrooms where all students feel valued, respected, and empowered to thrive academically and personally.

Domain 3: Instructional Delivery and Facilitation

Teaching Methods and Strategies

Candidates in Domain 3 embark on an exploration of diverse teaching methods and instructional strategies aimed at facilitating student learning and engagement. They delve into pedagogical approaches such as direct instruction, inquiry-based learning, cooperative learning, and project-based learning, among others. Candidates learn to differentiate instruction to meet the varied needs and learning styles of students, adapting teaching approaches and materials to ensure accessibility and inclusivity. They develop proficiency in creating engaging and interactive learning experiences that foster critical thinking, creativity, and collaboration among students. Through practical applications and reflective practices, candidates hone their skills in designing and delivering effective instruction that promotes deep understanding and meaningful learning outcomes.

Technology Integration in Education

This section immerses candidates in the world of educational technology and its transformative potential in teaching and learning. Candidates explore a range of educational technologies, including interactive whiteboards, multimedia presentations, educational software, and online learning platforms. They develop digital literacy skills and explore best practices for integrating technology seamlessly into instruction to enhance engagement, promote active learning, and facilitate collaboration among students. Candidates also learn to leverage technology to differentiate instruction, provide personalized learning experiences, and address diverse student needs. Moreover, they explore strategies for promoting digital citizenship and responsible use of technology, equipping students with the skills and competencies necessary for success in the digital age.

Monitoring and Assessing Student Progress

Candidates in this domain learn to monitor student progress and assess learning outcomes effectively to inform instructional decision-making. They explore a variety of assessment strategies, including formative assessments, summative assessments, and performance assessments. Candidates learn to use assessment data to identify students' strengths and areas for growth, provide timely and constructive feedback, and adjust instruction to meet individual learning needs. They develop proficiency in analyzing assessment results, interpreting data trends, and using evidence-based practices to optimize student learning. Through ongoing assessment, feedback, and reflection, candidates continuously refine their instructional practices to meet the evolving needs of students and promote academic achievement.

In summary, Domain 3 equips candidates with the knowledge, skills, and competencies necessary to deliver effective instruction and facilitate meaningful learning experiences. Through mastery of teaching methods and strategies, technology integration, and monitoring and assessment practices, candidates create dynamic and engaging learning environments that empower students to succeed academically and thrive in a rapidly evolving world.

Domain 4: Assessment Strategies

Types of Assessments

Candidates in Domain 4 delve into the diverse landscape of assessment types, understanding their unique purposes, characteristics, and applications in educational settings. They explore a variety of assessment methods, including formative assessments designed to monitor student progress and provide ongoing feedback, summative assessments used to evaluate student achievement at the conclusion of a unit or course, diagnostic assessments aimed at identifying students' strengths and areas for growth, and authentic assessments that mirror real-world tasks and scenarios. Candidates learn to select appropriate assessment methods based on learning objectives, student needs, and instructional contexts, ensuring alignment with instructional goals and promoting meaningful learning experiences for all students.

Data Analysis and Interpretation

This section focuses on equipping candidates with the skills and competencies necessary to analyze and interpret assessment data effectively. Candidates learn to collect, organize, and analyze assessment results using various data analysis techniques and tools. They develop proficiency in identifying trends, patterns, and outliers in assessment data, extracting meaningful insights to inform instructional decision-making. Candidates also explore strategies for synthesizing assessment data from multiple sources, such as standardized tests, classroom assessments, and student work samples, to gain a comprehensive understanding of student learning outcomes. By leveraging assessment data, candidates can evaluate student progress, identify areas of strength and growth, and make informed adjustments to instructional practices to optimize student learning and achievement.

Using Assessment for Feedback and Improvement

Candidates in this domain explore the pivotal role of assessment in providing feedback and fostering student growth. They learn to provide constructive feedback to students that is specific, actionable, and supportive, helping students understand their strengths and areas for improvement. Candidates also explore strategies for using assessment data to identify areas for instructional improvement, such as modifying instructional strategies, adjusting pacing or content delivery, or providing additional support or enrichment opportunities. Moreover, candidates learn to foster a culture of continuous learning and development, both for themselves and their students, by utilizing assessment as a tool for reflection, goal-setting, and improvement. By integrating assessment seamlessly into the instructional process, candidates create learning environments that promote academic excellence, student engagement, and personal growth.

In summary, Domain 4 equips candidates with the knowledge, skills, and dispositions necessary to design, implement, and interpret assessments effectively. Through mastery of assessment types, data analysis, and feedback strategies, candidates empower themselves and their students to achieve academic success, foster continuous improvement, and reach their full potential as learners and educators.

Domain 5: Professional Development and Ethical Practice

Continuing Professional Development

Candidates in Domain 5 delve into the dynamic realm of professional development and its paramount importance in the field of education. They recognize that education is a lifelong journey of learning and growth, and they explore various avenues for professional growth and advancement. Candidates examine opportunities for continuing education, such as workshops, conferences, seminars, and graduate coursework, where they can deepen their knowledge, refine their skills, and stay abreast of the latest research and best practices in education. They develop a commitment to ongoing professional development, recognizing its transformative impact on their practice and their ability to meet the evolving needs of students in a rapidly changing world.

Legal and Ethical Aspects of Teaching

This section immerses candidates in the complex and multifaceted landscape of legal and ethical responsibilities that accompany the teaching profession. Candidates explore ethical principles, such as integrity, honesty, and respect for diversity, as well as legal requirements and regulations governing education. They confront ethical dilemmas commonly encountered in educational settings and develop strategies for ethical decision-making that prioritize the well-being and rights of students. Candidates also familiarize themselves with professional codes of conduct and ethical guidelines, understanding their role in upholding the highest standards of professionalism and integrity in their practice.

Collaborative Relationships with Colleagues and Community

Candidates recognize the integral role of collaboration and teamwork in fostering a supportive and nurturing learning environment. They explore strategies for building positive and collaborative relationships with colleagues, parents, and community stakeholders to support student success and promote a positive school culture. Candidates learn effective communication skills, conflict resolution strategies, and techniques for fostering a culture of trust, respect, and mutual support among all members of the school community. They recognize the importance of parent and community involvement in education and explore ways to engage stakeholders in meaningful partnerships that enhance student learning and well-being.

In summary, Domain 5 underscores the importance of ongoing professional development and ethical practice in the teaching profession. Through mastery of these domains, candidates demonstrate a commitment to lifelong learning, ethical decision-making, and collaborative leadership, essential qualities for fostering student success and creating inclusive and supportive learning environments. By embracing these principles, educators empower themselves and their colleagues to continually strive for excellence and make a positive impact on the lives of their students and communities.

Building Bridges, Igniting Minds: The Promise of Educator Mastery

By immersing themselves fully into each domain with thoroughness and dedication, candidates acquire a profound comprehension of the breadth and depth of knowledge, as well as the array of skills and attitudes required to excel as educators in the vibrant educational landscape of Florida. Through rigorous study and practical application, educators emerge equipped with a multifaceted toolkit that enables them to navigate the complexities of teaching with confidence and proficiency.

With mastery of these domains, educators not only fulfill the requirements for certification but also embody the essence of effective teaching. They possess the pedagogical prowess to engage and inspire students, the strategic acumen to tailor instruction to diverse learning needs, and the empathetic understanding to create inclusive and nurturing learning environments.

Moreover, educators become agents of positive change within the educational community, wielding their expertise to uplift and empower students from all backgrounds. They serve as catalysts for growth and development, igniting a passion for lifelong learning and instilling in students the skills and values essential for success in an ever-evolving world.

By embracing the principles and practices embodied in these domains, educators transcend the role of mere instructors to become transformative leaders in education. They foster a culture of excellence, collaboration, and innovation, driving continuous improvement and progress within their schools and communities.

Ultimately, mastery of these domains not only signifies professional competence but also signifies a commitment to the noble cause of education. Educators emerge as champions of knowledge, advocates for equity, and architects of a brighter future for the next generation. Through their dedication and expertise, they leave an indelible mark on the lives of their students and contribute profoundly to the advancement of the educational community as a whole.

Chapter 4
Practice Questions and Answers

The FTCE Professional Education Test typically consists of approximately 120 multiple-choice questions. However, it's essential to check the specific requirements and format of the test as they may vary.

In this chapter, we've provided a few different mini practice tests to help prepare you to take the exam. You can use these tests to assess your understanding of key concepts and identify areas for further study. Each question will include the appropriate answer, as well as an explanation.

Strategies for Analyzing and Answering Practice Questions

Practice questions are an invaluable tool for preparing for the FTCE Professional Education Test. However, to make the most of your practice sessions, it's essential to approach them strategically. Here are some effective strategies for analyzing and answering practice questions:

Read the Question Carefully

Before you even look at the answer choices, take the time to thoroughly read and understand the question. Pay close attention to keywords, phrases, and any specific details provided.

Identify Key Information

Once you understand the question, identify any key information that is provided. This might include names, dates, numbers, or specific terms related to the topic being tested.

Break Down Complex Questions

If a question seems long or complicated, break it down into smaller parts. Focus on understanding each component individually before trying to tackle the question as a whole.

Eliminate Wrong Answers

After reading the question, eliminate any answer choices that are clearly incorrect. This can help narrow down your options and increase the likelihood of selecting the correct answer.

Use Process of Elimination

If you're unsure about an answer, use the process of elimination to rule out options that are unlikely to be correct. This can help you make an educated guess if you're stuck between multiple choices.

Look for Clues in the Question

Sometimes, the question itself contains clues or hints that can lead you to the correct answer. Pay attention to words or phrases that provide context or direction.

Consider All Options

Before making your final choice, carefully consider all answer options. Even if you think you know the correct answer, take a moment to review all choices to ensure you're not overlooking a better option.

Review Your Work

Once you've selected an answer, review your work to ensure it makes sense in the context of the question. Double-check for any errors or oversights before moving on to the next question.

Practice Active Reading

Engage actively with the practice questions by asking yourself questions about the content, making predictions, and trying to anticipate the answer before looking at the options.

Reflect on Mistakes

If you get a practice question wrong, take the time to understand why. Was it a misunderstanding of the content, a misinterpretation of the question, or a careless error? Learning from your mistakes is key to improvement.

By incorporating these strategies into your practice routine, you can develop the skills and confidence needed to tackle the FTCE Professional Education Test effectively. Remember to approach each practice question thoughtfully and methodically, using them as opportunities to strengthen your understanding and test-taking abilities.

Now, let's get into the practice tests!

Practice Test 1

Domain 1: Foundational Knowledge

1. Which learning theory emphasizes the role of reinforcement in shaping behavior?
    A) Constructivism
    B) Behaviorism
    C) Cognitivism
    D) Humanism

Correct Answer: B) Behaviorism

Explanation: Behaviorism focuses on observable behaviors and the role of reinforcement in learning.

2. According to Piaget's theory of cognitive development, which stage is characterized by the ability to think logically about concrete events?

A) Sensorimotor
B) Preoperational
C) Concrete operational
D) Formal operational

Correct Answer: C) Concrete operational

Explanation: The concrete operational stage, occurring from ages 7 to 11, is characterized by the ability to think logically about concrete events and grasp concrete analogies.

3. In curriculum development, what does the term "scope" refer to?

A) The depth of content covered in a curriculum
B) The breadth of content covered in a curriculum
C) The sequence of learning activities
D) The alignment with educational standards

Correct Answer: B) The breadth of content covered in a curriculum

Explanation: Scope refers to the breadth or range of content covered in a curriculum.

4. Which of the following is an example of a formative assessment?

A) Final exam
B) Midterm project
C) Classroom discussion
D) Standardized test

Correct Answer: C) Classroom discussion

Explanation: Formative assessments are ongoing assessments used to monitor student learning and provide feedback for instructional adjustments.

5. What is the primary purpose of diagnostic assessment?

A) To evaluate student performance at the end of a unit

B) To measure student achievement against learning standards

C) To identify students' strengths and weaknesses prior to instruction

D) To provide feedback on student progress

Correct Answer: C) To identify students' strengths and weaknesses prior to instruction

Explanation: Diagnostic assessments are used to assess students' prior knowledge, skills, and misconceptions before instruction begins.

6. Which ethical principle emphasizes honesty, integrity, and fairness in professional practice?

A) Autonomy

B) Beneficence

C) Nonmaleficence

D) Veracity

Correct Answer: D) Veracity

Explanation: Veracity refers to honesty, truthfulness, and accuracy in professional practice.

What is a key component of effective classroom management?

A) Punishing students for misbehavior
B) Establishing clear expectations and routines
C) Ignoring disruptive behavior
D) Avoiding interactions with students

Correct Answer: B) Establishing clear expectations and routines

Explanation: Clear expectations and routines help create a positive and structured learning environment.

Which of the following strategies can help promote student motivation?
A) Providing extrinsic rewards for all tasks
B) Offering choice and autonomy in learning tasks
C) Punishing students for mistakes
D) Focusing solely on competition among students

Correct Answer: B) Offering choice and autonomy in learning tasks

Explanation: Offering choice and autonomy in learning tasks can enhance intrinsic motivation and engagement.

What is the term for the integration of technology into teaching and learning?
A) Technology immersion
B) Digital literacy
C) Technology integration
D) Multimedia enhancement

Correct Answer: C) Technology integration

Explanation: Technology integration refers to the intentional use of technology to enhance teaching and learning experiences.

Which legal requirement ensures that students with

disabilities receive appropriate educational services and accommodations?

A) No Child Left Behind Act (NCLB)
B) Individuals with Disabilities Education Act (IDEA)
C) Every Student Succeeds Act (ESSA)
D) Americans with Disabilities Act (ADA)

Correct Answer: B) Individuals with Disabilities Education Act (IDEA)

Explanation: IDEA mandates that students with disabilities receive a free and appropriate public education (FAPE) tailored to their individual needs.

Domain 2: Student Development and Learning

Which of the following is an example of a milestone in physical development during early childhood?

A) Learning to read and write
B) Developing fine motor skills such as drawing
C) Acquiring abstract reasoning skills
D) Establishing personal identity

Correct Answer: B) Developing fine motor skills such as drawing

Explanation: Fine motor skills, such as drawing, are a common milestone in physical development during early childhood.

According to Erik Erikson's theory of psychosocial development, which stage occurs during adolescence and is characterized by the search for identity?

A) Trust vs. mistrust
B) Autonomy vs. shame and doubt
C) Initiative vs. guilt
D) Identity vs. role confusion

Correct Answer: D) Identity vs. role confusion

Explanation: The stage of identity vs. role confusion occurs during adolescence and is characterized by the exploration of personal identity.

Which of the following best describes the concept of zone of proximal development (ZPD) according to Lev Vygotsky?

A) The level of difficulty of tasks that a student can perform independently

B) The range of tasks that are too easy or too difficult for a student to complete

C) The difference between what a student can do independently and what they can do with assistance

D) The rate at which a student progresses through learning tasks

Correct Answer: C) The difference between what a student can do independently and what they can do with assistance

Explanation: The ZPD refers to the difference between what a student can do independently and what they can do with the assistance of a more knowledgeable other.

Which learning theory emphasizes the role of observation and imitation in learning?

A) Behaviorism
B) Cognitivism
C) Constructivism
D) Social learning theory

Correct Answer: D) Social learning theory

Explanation: Social learning theory,

proposed by Albert Bandura, emphasizes the role of observation and imitation in learning.

What is the primary function of the prefrontal cortex in the brain?

A) Processing sensory information
B) Regulating emotions and impulse control
C) Controlling motor movements
D) Storing long-term memories

Correct Answer: B) Regulating emotions and impulse control

Explanation: The prefrontal cortex is involved in higher-order cognitive functions such as regulating emotions, decision-making, and impulse control.

Which of the following statements best describes the role of culture in human development?

A) Culture has little to no impact on human development.
B) Culture shapes human development through socialization and learning.
C) Human development is solely determined by genetics.
D) Culture has a minor influence on human development.

Correct Answer: B) Culture shapes human development through socialization and learning.

Explanation: Culture plays a significant role in shaping human development through socialization, learning, and the transmission of values, beliefs, and practices.

Which of the following statements best describes the concept of scaffolding in the context of learning?

A) Providing support and guidance to help learners reach higher levels of understanding

B) Allowing learners to work independently without assistance

C) Presenting challenging tasks beyond learners' current abilities

D) Evaluating learners' performance based on predetermined criteria

Correct Answer: A) Providing support and guidance to help learners reach higher levels of understanding

Explanation: Scaffolding involves providing support and guidance to learners as they work on tasks, gradually reducing assistance as they develop competence.

What term refers to the ability to understand and manage one's own emotions and the emotions of others?

A) Emotional intelligence
B) Emotional regulation
C) Empathy
D) Social cognition

Correct Answer: A) Emotional intelligence

Explanation: Emotional intelligence refers to the ability to understand and manage one's own emotions and the emotions of others.

Which of the following is a characteristic of the adolescent brain?

A) Fully developed prefrontal cortex
B) Heightened risk-taking behavior
C) Stable neural connections
D) Decreased sensitivity to peer influence

Correct Answer: B) Heightened risk-taking behavior

Explanation: Adolescents often engage in heightened risk-taking behavior due to ongoing brain development and increased sensitivity to rewards.

According to Maslow's hierarchy of needs, which needs must be met before individuals can strive for self-actualization?

A) Physiological needs
B) Safety needs
C) Esteem needs
D) Belongingness and love needs

Correct Answer: A) Physiological needs

Explanation: According to Maslow, physiological needs such as food, water, and shelter must be met before individuals can strive for higher-level needs such as belongingness, esteem, and self-actualization.

Domain 3: Instructional Delivery & Facilitation

What is the primary goal of the think-aloud strategy in the classroom?

A) To encourage students to think silently about a concept
B) To help students develop metacognitive awareness by verbalizing their thought processes
C) To provide direct instruction on a topic
D) To assess students' understanding of a concept

Correct Answer: B) To help students develop metacognitive awareness by verbalizing their thought processes

Explanation: The think-aloud strategy involves students verbalizing their thought processes while solving problems or completing tasks, helping them develop metacognitive awareness and self-monitoring skills.

Which instructional strategy involves providing students with opportunities for self-directed learning and exploration?

A) Direct instruction
B) Inquiry-based learning
C) Recitation
D) Drill and practice

Correct Answer: B) Inquiry-based learning

Explanation: Inquiry-based learning empowers students to explore topics of interest through questioning, investigation, and discovery, promoting curiosity and independent learning.

What is the primary purpose of a rubric in the learning process?

A) To assign grades to students' work
B) To provide feedback to students on their performance
C) To assess students' prior knowledge before a lesson
D) To summarize key concepts learned during a lesson

Correct Answer: B) To provide feedback to students on their performance

Explanation: Rubrics are scoring guides used to provide clear criteria for assessing students' work and offering feedback on their performance.

Which instructional strategy involves providing

students with opportunities for hands-on experimentation and exploration?

A) Direct instruction
B) Experiential learning
C) Recitation
D) Drill and practice

Correct Answer: B) Experiential learning

Explanation: Experiential learning engages students in hands-on experiences and real-world applications of concepts, promoting active engagement and deeper understanding.

What is the primary goal of the gradual release model in instruction?

A) To eliminate student autonomy and independence
B) To shift responsibility for learning from students to the teacher
C) To gradually transfer responsibility for learning from the teacher to the students
D) To minimize student engagement in the learning process

Correct Answer: C) To gradually transfer responsibility for learning from the teacher to the students

Explanation: The gradual release model involves the teacher initially leading instruction and gradually transferring responsibility for learning to the students, promoting independence and self-directed learning.

Which instructional approach emphasizes the importance of providing students with opportunities for cooperative learning and peer interaction?

A) Behaviorism

B) Constructivism
C) Direct instruction
D) Social constructivism

Correct Answer: D) Social constructivism

Explanation: Social constructivism emphasizes the role of social interaction and collaboration in learning, with a focus on cooperative learning and peer interaction.

What is the primary purpose of a gallery walk activity in the classroom?

A) To limit student interaction during lessons
B) To promote competition among students
C) To encourage peer review and feedback on student work
D) To discourage collaboration and teamwork

Correct Answer: C) To encourage peer review and feedback on student work

Explanation: A gallery walk involves students circulating around the classroom to view and provide feedback on each other's work, promoting peer review, collaboration, and reflection.

Which instructional strategy involves providing students with opportunities for choice and autonomy in their learning?

A) Direct instruction
B) Differentiated instruction
C) Project-based learning
D) Recitation

Correct Answer: B) Differentiated instruction

Explanation: Differentiated instruction involves adjusting instruction to meet the diverse learning needs, interests, and readiness levels of individual students, often providing choice and autonomy in learning activities.

What is the primary goal of a peer tutoring program in the classroom?

A) To limit student interaction during lessons
B) To promote competition among students
C) To foster collaboration and peer teaching
D) To discourage collaboration and teamwork

Correct Answer: C) To foster collaboration and peer teaching

Explanation: *Peer tutoring programs involve students teaching and supporting each other, promoting collaboration, peer teaching, and mutual learning.*

Which instructional strategy involves providing students with opportunities for reflection and self-assessment of their learning?

A) Direct instruction
B) Reciprocal teaching
C) Metacognitive strategies
D) Drill and practice

Correct Answer: C) Metacognitive strategies

Explanation: *Metacognitive strategies involve students reflecting on and monitoring their own learning processes, promoting self-awareness, and self-assessment.*

Domain 4: Assessment Strategies

Which type of assessment is typically conducted before instruction begins to gauge students' prior knowledge, skills, and understanding of a topic?

A) Formative assessment

B) Summative assessment

C) Diagnostic assessment

D) Authentic assessment

Correct Answer: C) Diagnostic assessment

Explanation: Diagnostic assessments are used to diagnose students' strengths, weaknesses, and prior knowledge before instruction begins.

What is the primary purpose of formative assessment?

A) To evaluate students' mastery of content at the end of instruction

B) To provide ongoing feedback to students to guide learning and improvement

C) To assign grades to students' work

D) To measure students' overall achievement at the end of a unit or course

Correct Answer: B) To provide ongoing feedback to students to guide learning and improvement

Explanation: Formative assessment is used during instruction to provide feedback to students and guide their learning process.

Which type of assessment is typically administered after instruction to evaluate students' overall mastery of content and learning objectives?

A) Formative assessment

B) Summative assessment

C) Diagnostic assessment

D) Authentic assessment

Correct Answer: B) Summative assessment

Explanation: Summative assessments are used to evaluate students' overall mastery of

content and learning objectives after instruction has occurred.

What is the primary purpose of authentic assessment?

A) To measure students' memorization of facts and information

B) To provide opportunities for students to apply their learning in real-world contexts

C) To assign grades to students' work

D) To assess students' overall achievement at the end of a unit or course

Correct Answer: B) To provide opportunities for students to apply their learning in real-world contexts

Explanation: Authentic assessment tasks mirror real-world situations and require students to apply their learning in authentic contexts.

Which assessment technique involves students responding to a series of questions or prompts in writing?

A) Performance assessment

B) Portfolio assessment

C) Essay assessment

D) Rubric assessment

Correct Answer: C) Essay assessment

Explanation: Essay assessments require students to respond to questions or prompts in writing, demonstrating their understanding and knowledge of a topic.

What is the primary purpose of performance assessment?

A) To measure students' memorization of facts and information

B) To provide opportunities for students to demonstrate skills and abilities in real-world tasks or scenarios

C) To assign grades to students' work

D) To assess students' overall achievement at the end of a unit or course

Correct Answer: B) To provide opportunities for students to demonstrate skills and abilities in real-world tasks or scenarios

Explanation: Performance assessments require students to demonstrate their skills and abilities in authentic tasks or scenarios.

Which type of assessment allows students to compile a collection of their work to demonstrate their learning and progress over time?

A) Formative assessment

B) Summative assessment

C) Diagnostic assessment

D) Portfolio assessment

Correct Answer: D) Portfolio assessment

Explanation: Portfolio assessments allow students to compile a collection of their work to demonstrate their learning and progress over time.

What is the primary purpose of a rubric in assessment?

A) To measure students' memorization of facts and information

B) To provide feedback to students on their performance

C) To assign grades to students' work

D) To assess students' overall achievement at the end of a unit or course

Correct Answer: B) To provide feedback to students on their performance

Explanation: Rubrics are scoring guides used to provide clear criteria for assessing students' work and offering feedback on their performance.

Which assessment technique involves students selecting their best work to showcase their learning and achievement?

A) Performance assessment
B) Portfolio assessment
C) Essay assessment
D) Rubric assessment

Correct Answer: B) Portfolio assessment

Explanation: Portfolio assessment involves students selecting their best work to showcase their learning and achievement over time.

Which type of assessment is typically conducted throughout instruction to monitor students' progress and inform instructional decision-making?

A) Formative assessment
B) Summative assessment
C) Diagnostic assessment
D) Authentic assessment

Correct Answer: A) Formative assessment

Explanation: Formative assessment is used throughout instruction to monitor students' progress and provide feedback to guide learning and instruction.

Domain 5: Professional Development &

Ethical Practice

What is the primary purpose of engaging in continuing professional development as an educator?

A) To fulfill mandatory training requirements
B) To earn higher salaries and bonuses
C) To enhance teaching skills and knowledge
D) To decrease workload and stress levels

Answer: C) To enhance teaching skills and knowledge

Explanation: Continuing professional development helps educators stay current with advancements in their field, acquire new teaching strategies, and improve their effectiveness in the classroom.

Which of the following is an example of a professional code of conduct for educators?

A) The Hippocratic Oath
B) The Nuremberg Code
C) The National Education Association Code of Ethics
D) The Magna Carta

Answer: C) The National Education Association Code of Ethics

Explanation: The National Education Association (NEA) Code of Ethics outlines the ethical standards and principles that educators should uphold in their professional practice.

What is the purpose of legal requirements for educators in the teaching profession?

A) To restrict educators' freedom of expression
B) To ensure compliance with state and federal laws
C) To promote inequality and discrimination
D) To discourage educators from seeking professional

development

Answer: B) To ensure compliance with state and federal laws

Explanation: Legal requirements for educators aim to ensure that educators adhere to laws and regulations governing education, protecting the rights and well-being of students.

Which of the following is an ethical dilemma commonly faced by educators?

A) Choosing a favorite student to receive special treatment

B) Falsifying student test scores to meet performance targets

C) Encouraging students to cheat on exams

D) Allowing bullying behavior to go unaddressed in the classroom

Answer: D) Allowing bullying behavior to go unaddressed in the classroom

Explanation: Allowing bullying behavior to persist presents an ethical dilemma for educators as they must balance their duty to maintain a safe and inclusive learning environment with concerns about student privacy and confidentiality.

How does engaging in continuing professional development benefit educators and students?

A) It increases workload and stress levels for educators

B) It provides opportunities for educators to earn higher salaries

C) It enhances teaching skills and knowledge, leading to improved student outcomes

D) It restricts educators' freedom of expression in the

classroom

Answer: C) It enhances teaching skills and knowledge, leading to improved student outcomes

Explanation: Engaging in continuing professional development allows educators to enhance their teaching skills and knowledge, ultimately benefiting students by improving the quality of instruction and learning experiences.

Which of the following is an example of a collaborative relationship with colleagues?

A) Competing with colleagues for recognition and rewards

B) Sharing teaching strategies and resources with colleagues

C) Ignoring colleagues' input and feedback

D) Refusing to collaborate on team projects or initiatives

Answer: B) Sharing teaching strategies and resources with colleagues

Explanation: Collaborative relationships with colleagues involve sharing ideas, resources, and expertise to enhance teaching practices and support student learning.

What role do educators play in promoting social justice and equity in education?

A) To perpetuate inequality and discrimination

B) To maintain the status quo and uphold existing power structures

C) To advocate for fairness, inclusivity, and equal opportunities for all students

D) To prioritize the needs of privileged students over

marginalized groups

Answer: C) To advocate for fairness, inclusivity, and equal opportunities for all students

Explanation: Educators have a responsibility to advocate for social justice and equity in education by ensuring that all students have access to quality education and opportunities for success, regardless of their background or circumstances.

How does collaborative engagement with parents and community stakeholders benefit the education system?

A) It limits parental involvement in the education process

B) It fosters a sense of partnership and shared responsibility for student success

C) It creates a barrier between the school and the surrounding community

D) It excludes parents and community members from decision-making processes

Answer: B) It fosters a sense of partnership and shared responsibility for student success

Explanation: Collaborative engagement with parents and community stakeholders fosters a sense of partnership and shared responsibility for student success, leading to improved outcomes and a stronger sense of community within the education system.

Which of the following is an example of a legal requirement for educators?

A) Encouraging students to engage in risky behaviors

B) Violating students' privacy rights by sharing confidential information

C) Providing a safe and inclusive learning environment for all students

D) Fostering a supportive and nurturing classroom climate

Answer: C) Providing a safe and inclusive learning environment for all students

Explanation: Educators are legally required to provide a safe and inclusive learning environment for all students, free from discrimination, harassment, and harm.

What is the significance of ethical decision-making in the teaching profession?

A) It allows educators to prioritize their own interests over those of students

B) It ensures compliance with state and federal laws governing education

C) It promotes integrity, honesty, and professionalism in educator-student interactions

D) It restricts educators' freedom of expression in the classroom

Answer: C) It promotes integrity, honesty, and professionalism in educator-student interactions

Explanation: Ethical decision-making is essential in the teaching profession as it promotes integrity, honesty, and professionalism in educator-student interactions, contributing to a positive learning environment and fostering trust and respect between educators and students.

Chapter 5
Practice Test 2

Domain 1: Foundational Knowledge
Which of the following learning theories emphasizes the role of intrinsic motivation and self-directed learning?
A) Behaviorism
B) Cognitivism
C) Constructivism
D) Humanism
Correct Answer: D) Humanism
Explanation: Humanism emphasizes intrinsic motivation, self-directed learning, and the importance of personal growth and fulfillment.

According to Piaget's theory of cognitive development, which stage is characterized by the ability to think abstractly and logically?
A) Sensorimotor
B) Preoperational

C) Concrete operational
D) Formal operational

Correct Answer: D) Formal operational

Explanation: The formal operational stage, occurring from adolescence to adulthood, is characterized by the ability to think abstractly and logically.

Which of the following best describes the concept of schema in cognitive development?

A) Inborn, biologically determined patterns of behavior
B) Mental frameworks for organizing and interpreting information
C) Learned associations between stimuli and responses
D) Units of hereditary information transmitted from parents to offspring

Correct Answer: B) Mental frameworks for organizing and interpreting information

Explanation: Schemas are mental frameworks or structures that organize and interpret information in the environment.

What is the primary purpose of summative assessment?

A) To monitor student progress and provide ongoing feedback
B) To diagnose students' strengths and weaknesses prior to instruction
C) To evaluate student achievement at the end of a unit or course
D) To promote student engagement and motivation

Correct Answer: C) To evaluate student achievement at the end of a unit or course

Explanation: Summative assessments are

used to evaluate student learning outcomes at the end of a unit, course, or instructional period.

Which of the following best describes the concept of assimilation in cognitive development?

A) The process of incorporating new information into existing schemas

B) The process of modifying existing schemas to accommodate new information

C) The process of forming new schemas in response to novel experiences

D) The process of unlearning previously acquired knowledge

Correct Answer: A) The process of incorporating new information into existing schemas

Explanation: Assimilation involves incorporating new information into existing schemas or mental frameworks.

Which ethical principle emphasizes the importance of confidentiality and trust in professional relationships?

A) Autonomy
B) Nonmaleficence
C) Veracity
D) Confidentiality

Correct Answer: D) Confidentiality

Explanation: Confidentiality is an ethical principle that emphasizes the importance of privacy, trust, and confidentiality in professional relationships.

Which of the following is a proactive classroom management strategy?

A) Reacting to misbehavior after it occurs
B) Establishing clear expectations and rules
C) Ignoring disruptive behavior
D) Punishing students for mistakes

Correct Answer: B) Establishing clear expectations and rules

Explanation: Proactive classroom management involves establishing clear expectations, rules, and routines to prevent misbehavior before it occurs.

What is the term for providing students with choices and opportunities for autonomy in learning tasks?
A) Differentiation
B) Personalization
C) Individualization
D) Autonomy

Correct Answer: D) Autonomy

Explanation: Autonomy refers to providing students with choices and opportunities for self-direction in learning tasks.

Which of the following is an example of an authentic assessment?
A) Multiple-choice test
B) Standardized test
C) Portfolio assessment
D) True-false test

Correct Answer: C) Portfolio assessment

Explanation: Portfolio assessment involves the collection and evaluation of student work samples over time to demonstrate learning and growth.

Which federal law mandates equal access to education for students with disabilities?
A) No Child Left Behind Act (NCLB)
B) Individuals with Disabilities Education Act (IDEA)
C) Every Student Succeeds Act (ESSA)
D) Americans with Disabilities Act (ADA)

Correct Answer: B) Individuals with Disabilities Education Act (IDEA)

Explanation: IDEA mandates that students with disabilities receive a free and appropriate public education (FAPE) tailored to their individual needs.

Domain 2: Student Development and Learning

Which of the following best describes the concept of nature versus nurture in human development?
A) The relative contributions of genetics and environment to human behavior and development
B) The role of heredity in shaping individual differences in behavior and personality
C) The influence of peers and social interactions on human development
D) The impact of culture on cognitive development and learning

Correct Answer: A) The relative contributions of genetics and environment to human behavior and development

Explanation: Nature versus nurture refers to the debate over the relative contributions of genetics (nature) and environment (nurture) to human behavior and development.

According to Erik Erikson's theory of psychosocial

development, which stage occurs during infancy and is characterized by the development of trust and mistrust?

A) Autonomy vs. shame and doubt
B) Trust vs. mistrust
C) Initiative vs. guilt
D) Industry vs. inferiority

Correct Answer: B) Trust vs. mistrust

Explanation: The stage of trust vs. mistrust occurs during infancy and is characterized by the development of trust in caregivers.

Which of the following best describes the concept of conservation in Piaget's theory of cognitive development?

A) The ability to understand that changes in appearance do not change the quantity of an object
B) The understanding that objects continue to exist even when they are not visible
C) The ability to understand the perspectives of others and take them into account
D) The understanding that certain characteristics of objects remain the same despite changes in appearance

Correct Answer: D) The understanding that certain characteristics of objects remain the same despite changes in appearance

Explanation: Conservation refers to the understanding that certain characteristics of objects, such as quantity, volume, and mass, remain the same despite changes in appearance.

Which of the following best describes the concept of egocentrism in Piaget's theory of cognitive development?

A) The ability to understand the perspectives of others
B) The tendency to focus exclusively on one's own point of view and ignore others' perspectives

C) The understanding that objects continue to exist even when they are not visible

D) The ability to understand that changes in appearance do not change the quantity of an object

Correct Answer: B) The tendency to focus exclusively on one's own point of view and ignore others' perspectives

Explanation: Egocentrism is the tendency to focus exclusively on one's own point of view and ignore or disregard others' perspectives.

Which of the following best describes the concept of assimilation in cognitive development?

A) The process of incorporating new information into existing schemas

B) The process of modifying existing schemas to accommodate new information

C) The process of forming new schemas in response to novel experiences

D) The process of unlearning previously acquired knowledge

Correct Answer: A) The process of incorporating new information into existing schemas

Explanation: Assimilation involves incorporating new information into existing schemas or mental frameworks.

Which of the following is a characteristic of the formal operational stage of cognitive development according to Piaget?

A) Concrete operational thinking
B) Abstract and logical reasoning
C) Egocentrism
D) Lack of conservation

Correct Answer: B) Abstract and logical reasoning

Explanation: The formal operational stage, occurring from adolescence to adulthood, is characterized by abstract and logical reasoning abilities.

Which of the following best describes the concept of zone of proximal development (ZPD) according to Lev Vygotsky?

A) The level of difficulty of tasks that a student can perform independently

B) The range of tasks that are too easy or too difficult for a student to complete

C) The difference between what a student can do independently and what they can do with assistance

D) The rate at which a student progresses through learning tasks

Correct Answer: C) The difference between what a student can do independently and what they can do with assistance

Explanation: The ZPD refers to the difference between what a student can do independently and what they can do with the assistance of a more knowledgeable other.

What is the term for the process of building on students' existing knowledge and experiences to facilitate learning?

A) Scaffolding
B) Differentiation
C) Accommodation
D) Assimilation

Correct Answer: A) Scaffolding

Explanation: Scaffolding involves providing

support and guidance to learners as they work on tasks, gradually reducing assistance as they develop competence.

Which of the following is a characteristic of the adolescent brain?

A) Fully developed prefrontal cortex
B) Heightened risk-taking behavior
C) Stable neural connections
D) Decreased sensitivity to peer influence

Correct Answer: B) Heightened risk-taking behavior

Explanation: Adolescents often engage in heightened risk-taking behavior due to ongoing brain development and increased sensitivity to rewards.

According to Maslow's hierarchy of needs, which needs must be met before individuals can strive for self-actualization?

A) Physiological needs
B) Safety needs
C) Esteem needs
D) Belongingness and love needs

Correct Answer: A) Physiological needs

Explanation: According to Maslow, physiological needs such as food, water, and shelter must be met before individuals can strive for higher-level needs such as belongingness, esteem, and self-actualization.

Domain 3: Instructional Delivery & Facilitation

Which instructional strategy involves incorporating

real-world examples, anecdotes, or analogies to illustrate abstract concepts and enhance student understanding?

A) Differentiated instruction
B) Experiential learning
C) Inquiry-based learning
D) Use of analogies

Correct Answer: D) Use of analogies

Explanation: Using analogies helps students relate abstract concepts to familiar real-world scenarios, facilitating comprehension and retention.

What is the purpose of a think-pair-share activity in the classroom?

A) To encourage individual reflection on a topic
B) To facilitate collaboration and peer discussion
C) To minimize student interaction during lessons
D) To assess students' understanding of a concept

Correct Answer: B) To facilitate collaboration and peer discussion

Explanation: Think-pair-share encourages students to think about a question or prompt individually, discuss their thoughts with a partner, and then share their ideas with the whole class, promoting collaboration and active participation.

Which instructional strategy involves gradually releasing responsibility for learning from the teacher to the students?

A) Direct instruction
B) Reciprocal teaching
C) Gradual release model
D) Cooperative learning

Correct Answer: C) Gradual release model

Explanation: The gradual release model involves the teacher initially demonstrating or modeling a concept, then guiding students through the learning process, and finally allowing students to practice independently.

What is the primary goal of reciprocal teaching?

A) To promote competition among students

B) To encourage individual achievement only

C) To foster collaboration and peer teaching

D) To minimize student engagement in the learning process

Correct Answer: C) To foster collaboration and peer teaching

Explanation: Reciprocal teaching involves students taking turns leading discussions and teaching each other, promoting collaboration, peer interaction, and deeper understanding of concepts.

Which instructional approach emphasizes the importance of students' prior knowledge and experiences in constructing new understanding?

A) Behaviorism

B) Constructivism

C) Direct instruction

D) Humanism

Correct Answer: B) Constructivism

Explanation: Constructivism is an instructional approach that emphasizes the active role of students in constructing their own under-

standing of concepts based on prior knowledge and experiences.

What is the purpose of metacognitive strategies in the learning process?

A) To memorize facts and information
B) To regulate and monitor one's own learning
C) To complete tasks quickly without reflection
D) To compete with peers for academic achievement

Correct Answer: B) To regulate and monitor one's own learning

Explanation: Metacognitive strategies involve regulating and monitoring one's own learning processes, such as planning, monitoring progress, and evaluating understanding.

Which instructional strategy involves providing students with opportunities to explore open-ended questions or problems, encouraging curiosity and inquiry?

A) Direct instruction
B) Inquiry-based learning
C) Drill and practice
D) Recitation

Correct Answer: B) Inquiry-based learning

Explanation: Inquiry-based learning involves posing open-ended questions or problems to students, encouraging curiosity, exploration, and critical thinking.

What is the primary goal of a jigsaw activity in the classroom?

A) To minimize student interaction during lessons
B) To promote competition among students
C) To foster collaboration and teamwork among students

D) To discourage peer learning

Correct Answer: C) To foster collaboration and teamwork among students

Explanation: Jigsaw activities involve dividing students into groups, with each group becoming experts on a specific topic or concept and then sharing their knowledge with the whole class, promoting collaboration and teamwork.

Which instructional approach emphasizes the importance of providing students with opportunities for hands-on, experiential learning?

A) Experiential learning
B) Behaviorism
C) Drill and practice
D) Lecture

Correct Answer: A) Experiential learning

Explanation: Experiential learning involves providing students with hands-on experiences and real-world applications of concepts to enhance learning and understanding.

What is the primary purpose of a concept map in the learning process?

A) To summarize key concepts learned during a lesson
B) To assess students' prior knowledge before a lesson
C) To organize and visually represent the relationships between concepts
D) To track students' progress on learning objectives

Correct Answer: C) To organize and visually represent the relationships between concepts

Explanation: Concept maps visually represent the relationships between concepts, helping students organize information, make connections, and enhance understanding.

Domain 4: Assessment Strategies

What is the primary purpose of a performance rubric in assessment?

A) To measure students' memorization of facts and information

B) To provide feedback to students on their performance

C) To assign grades to students' work

D) To assess students' overall achievement at the end of a unit or course

Correct Answer: B) To provide feedback to students on their performance

Explanation: Performance rubrics outline specific criteria for assessing students' performance on a task or project and provide feedback to students on their strengths and areas for improvement.

Which assessment technique involves observing students' behaviors and actions in authentic settings?

A) Performance assessment

B) Portfolio assessment

C) Essay assessment

D) Rubric assessment

Correct Answer: A) Performance assessment

Explanation: Performance assessment involves observing students' behaviors and actions as they engage in authentic tasks or activities, allowing for the assessment of skills and abilities in real-world contexts.

What is the primary purpose of a checklist in assessment?

A) To measure students' memorization of facts and information
B) To provide feedback to students on their performance
C) To assign grades to students' work
D) To track students' completion of specific tasks or criteria

Correct Answer: D) To track students' completion of specific tasks or criteria

Explanation: Checklists are used to track students' completion of specific tasks or criteria and provide a simple way to record whether students have met predetermined criteria.

Which assessment technique involves students completing a series of tasks or problems to demonstrate their understanding and skills?

A) Performance assessment
B) Portfolio assessment
C) Essay assessment
D) Rubric assessment

Correct Answer: A) Performance assessment

Explanation: Performance assessment requires students to complete tasks or problems to demonstrate their understanding and skills in real-world contexts.

What is the primary purpose of peer assessment in the classroom?

A) To assign grades to students' work
B) To provide opportunities for students to give and receive feedback on their peers' work

C) To minimize students' involvement in the assessment process

D) To evaluate students' mastery of content at the end of instruction

Correct Answer: B) To provide opportunities for students to give and receive feedback on their peers' work

Explanation: Peer assessment involves students providing feedback on their peers' work, promoting collaboration, peer learning, and reflection.

Which type of assessment involves students creating a physical or digital collection of their work to demonstrate their learning and progress?

A) Performance assessment

B) Portfolio assessment

C) Essay assessment

D) Rubric assessment

Correct Answer: B) Portfolio assessment

Explanation: Portfolio assessment requires students to compile a collection of their work to showcase their learning and progress over time.

What is the primary purpose of self-assessment in the learning process?

A) To assign grades to students' work

B) To provide opportunities for students to reflect on their own learning and progress

C) To minimize students' involvement in the assessment process

D) To evaluate students' mastery of content at the end of instruction

Correct Answer: B) To provide opportunities

for students to reflect on their own learning and progress

Explanation: Self-assessment involves students reflecting on their own learning and progress, identifying strengths and areas for improvement, and setting goals for future learning.

Which type of assessment involves students completing tasks or projects that simulate real-world challenges or scenarios?

A) Performance assessment
B) Portfolio assessment
C) Essay assessment
D) Rubric assessment

Correct Answer: A) Performance assessment

Explanation: Performance assessment tasks or projects simulate real-world challenges or scenarios, allowing students to demonstrate their skills and abilities in authentic contexts.

What is the primary purpose of a scoring guide in assessment?

A) To measure students' memorization of facts and information
B) To provide feedback to students on their performance
C) To assign grades to students' work
D) To assess students' overall achievement at the end of a unit or course

Correct Answer: C) To assign grades to students' work

Explanation: Scoring guides, or rubrics, outline specific criteria for assessing students' work and assigning grades based on predetermined standards.

Which assessment technique involves students reflecting on their learning experiences, accomplishments, and challenges?

A) Self-assessment
B) Peer assessment
C) Performance assessment
D) Portfolio assessment

Correct Answer: A) Self-assessment

Explanation: *Self-assessment involves students reflecting on their own learning experiences, accomplishments, and challenges, promoting self-awareness and metacognition.*

Domain 5: Professional Development & Ethical Practice

What is the purpose of continuing professional development for educators?

A) To decrease workload and stress levels
B) To fulfill mandatory training requirements
C) To enhance teaching skills and knowledge
D) To earn higher salaries and bonuses

Answer: C) To enhance teaching skills and knowledge

Explanation: *Continuing professional development helps educators improve their teaching skills, stay updated with new methodologies, and enhance student learning outcomes.*

Which of the following is a key aspect of ethical conduct in the teaching profession?

A) Prioritizing one's own interests over those of students
B) Engaging in discriminatory practices

C) Upholding confidentiality and respecting student privacy

D) Ignoring professional boundaries with students

Answer: C) Upholding confidentiality and respecting student privacy

Explanation: Ethical conduct in the teaching profession includes respecting student privacy and maintaining confidentiality to create a trusting and supportive learning environment.

How do legal requirements for educators contribute to ethical practice?

A) By promoting discrimination and inequality

B) By restricting educators' freedom of expression

C) By ensuring compliance with laws and regulations

D) By discouraging educators from seeking professional development

Answer: C) By ensuring compliance with laws and regulations

Explanation: Legal requirements for educators help ensure that they adhere to laws and regulations, promoting ethical practice and protecting the rights of students.

Which of the following is an example of a collaborative relationship with community stakeholders?

A) Ignoring input from parents and community members

B) Providing opportunities for community involvement in school activities

C) Refusing to collaborate on projects or initiatives with local organizations

D) Excluding parents and community members from decision-making processes

Answer: B) Providing opportunities for community involvement in school activities

Explanation: Collaborative relationships with community stakeholders involve engaging with parents and community members and providing opportunities for their involvement in school activities and decision-making processes.

Why is it important for educators to advocate for social justice and equity in education?

A) To perpetuate inequality and discrimination

B) To maintain the status quo and uphold existing power structures

C) To ensure equal opportunities for all students and address systemic barriers

D) To prioritize the needs of privileged students over marginalized groups

Answer: C) To ensure equal opportunities for all students and address systemic barriers

Explanation: Advocating for social justice and equity in education helps ensure that all students have equal opportunities for success and addresses systemic barriers that may hinder the achievement of marginalized groups.

How do collaborative relationships with colleagues benefit educators and students?

A) By increasing competition among educators

B) By fostering a sense of teamwork and cooperation

C) By limiting opportunities for professional growth and development

D) By excluding parents and community stakeholders from the education process

Answer: B) By fostering a sense of teamwork and cooperation

Explanation: *Collaborative relationships with colleagues promote teamwork, allowing educators to share ideas, resources, and best practices, ultimately benefiting student learning outcomes.*

What role does professional development play in promoting ethical practice?

A) It restricts educators' freedom of expression

B) It encourages unethical behavior

C) It enhances educators' understanding of ethical principles and standards

D) It decreases educators' accountability

Answer: C) It enhances educators' understanding of ethical principles and standards

Explanation: *Professional development helps educators deepen their understanding of ethical principles and standards, enabling them to make informed decisions and uphold ethical conduct in their professional practice.*

Why is it important for educators to maintain collaborative relationships with parents?

A) To limit parental involvement in the education process

B) To create a sense of exclusivity within the school community

C) To foster a partnership in supporting student learning and well-being

D) To prioritize educators' interests over those of students

***Answer:** C) To foster a partnership in supporting student learning and well-being*

***Explanation:** Collaborative relationships with parents create a partnership in supporting student learning and well-being, allowing educators and parents to work together towards common goals.*

Which of the following is an example of ethical conduct in the teaching profession?

A) Ignoring student privacy rights and confidentiality

B) Fostering a safe and inclusive learning environment for all students

C) Engaging in discriminatory practices based on student characteristics

D) Placing personal interests above the needs of students

***Answer:** B) Fostering a safe and inclusive learning environment for all students*

***Explanation:** Ethical conduct in the teaching profession involves fostering a safe and inclusive learning environment for all students, free from discrimination and harassment.*

How can educators demonstrate their commitment to ongoing professional development?

A) By resisting opportunities for growth and improvement

B) By attending workshops, conferences, and training sessions

C) By isolating themselves from colleagues and professional networks

D) By refusing to engage in self-reflection and continuous learning

Answer: B) By attending workshops, conferences, and training sessions

Explanation: Educators demonstrate their commitment to ongoing professional development by actively seeking opportunities for growth and improvement, such as attending workshops, conferences, and training sessions.

Chapter 6
Pactice Test 3

Domain 1: Foundational Knowledge
Which of the following learning theories emphasizes the role of intrinsic motivation and self-directed learning?
A) Behaviorism
B) Cognitivism
C) Constructivism
D) Humanism

Correct Answer: D) Humanism

Explanation: Humanism emphasizes intrinsic motivation, self-directed learning, and the importance of personal growth and fulfillment.

According to Piaget's theory of cognitive development, which stage is characterized by the ability to think abstractly and logically?
A) Sensorimotor
B) Preoperational
C) Concrete operational

D) Formal operational

Correct Answer: D) Formal operational

Explanation: The formal operational stage, occurring from adolescence to adulthood, is characterized by the ability to think abstractly and logically.

Which of the following best describes the concept of schema in cognitive development?

A) Inborn, biologically determined patterns of behavior

B) Mental frameworks for organizing and interpreting information

C) Learned associations between stimuli and responses

D) Units of hereditary information transmitted from parents to offspring

Correct Answer: B) Mental frameworks for organizing and interpreting information

Explanation: Schemas are mental frameworks or structures that organize and interpret information in the environment.

What is the primary purpose of summative assessment?

A) To monitor student progress and provide ongoing feedback

B) To diagnose students' strengths and weaknesses prior to instruction

C) To evaluate student achievement at the end of a unit or course

D) To promote student engagement and motivation

Correct Answer: C) To evaluate student achievement at the end of a unit or course

Explanation: Summative assessments are used to evaluate student learning outcomes at

the end of a unit, course, or instructional period.

Which of the following best describes the concept of assimilation in cognitive development?

A) The process of incorporating new information into existing schemas

B) The process of modifying existing schemas to accommodate new information

C) The process of forming new schemas in response to novel experiences

D) The process of unlearning previously acquired knowledge

Correct Answer: A) The process of incorporating new information into existing schemas

Explanation: Assimilation involves incorporating new information into existing schemas or mental frameworks.

Which ethical principle emphasizes the importance of confidentiality and trust in professional relationships?

A) Autonomy

B) Nonmaleficence

C) Veracity

D) Confidentiality

Correct Answer: D) Confidentiality

Explanation: Confidentiality is an ethical principle that emphasizes the importance of privacy, trust, and confidentiality in professional relationships.

Which of the following is a proactive classroom management strategy?

A) Reacting to misbehavior after it occurs

B) Establishing clear expectations and rules

C) Ignoring disruptive behavior
D) Punishing students for mistakes

Correct Answer: B) Establishing clear expectations and rules

Explanation: Proactive classroom management involves establishing clear expectations, rules, and routines to prevent misbehavior before it occurs.

What is the term for providing students with choices and opportunities for autonomy in learning tasks?
A) Differentiation
B) Personalization
C) Individualization
D) Autonomy

Correct Answer: D) Autonomy

Explanation: Autonomy refers to providing students with choices and opportunities for self-direction in learning tasks.

Which of the following is an example of an authentic assessment?
A) Multiple-choice test
B) Standardized test
C) Portfolio assessment
D) True-false test

Correct Answer: C) Portfolio assessment

Explanation: Portfolio assessment involves the collection and evaluation of student work samples over time to demonstrate learning and growth.

Which federal law mandates equal access to education for students with disabilities?
A) No Child Left Behind Act (NCLB)
B) Individuals with Disabilities Education Act (IDEA)

C) Every Student Succeeds Act (ESSA)
D) Americans with Disabilities Act (ADA)

Correct Answer: B) Individuals with Disabilities Education Act (IDEA)

Explanation: IDEA mandates that students with disabilities receive a free and appropriate public education (FAPE) tailored to their individual needs.

Domain 2: Student Development and Learning

Which of the following best describes the concept of nature versus nurture in human development?

A) The relative contributions of genetics and environment to human behavior and development

B) The role of heredity in shaping individual differences in behavior and personality

C) The influence of peers and social interactions on human development

D) The impact of culture on cognitive development and learning

Correct Answer: A) The relative contributions of genetics and environment to human behavior and development

Explanation: Nature versus nurture refers to the debate over the relative contributions of genetics (nature) and environment (nurture) to human behavior and development.

According to Erik Erikson's theory of psychosocial development, which stage occurs during infancy and is characterized by the development of trust and mistrust?

A) Autonomy vs. shame and doubt
B) Trust vs. mistrust

C) Initiative vs. guilt

D) Industry vs. inferiority

Correct Answer: B) Trust vs. mistrust

Explanation: The stage of trust vs. mistrust occurs during infancy and is characterized by the development of trust in caregivers.

Which of the following best describes the concept of conservation in Piaget's theory of cognitive development?

A) The ability to understand that changes in appearance do not change the quantity of an object

B) The understanding that objects continue to exist even when they are not visible

C) The ability to understand the perspectives of others and take them into account

D) The understanding that certain characteristics of objects remain the same despite changes in appearance

Correct Answer: D) The understanding that certain characteristics of objects remain the same despite changes in appearance

Explanation: Conservation refers to the understanding that certain characteristics of objects, such as quantity, volume, and mass, remain the same despite changes in appearance.

Which of the following best describes the concept of egocentrism in Piaget's theory of cognitive development?

A) The ability to understand the perspectives of others

B) The tendency to focus exclusively on one's own point of view and ignore others' perspectives

C) The understanding that objects continue to exist even when they are not visible

D) The ability to understand that changes in appearance do not change the quantity of an object

Correct Answer: B) The tendency to focus exclusively on one's own point of view and ignore others' perspectives

Explanation: Egocentrism is the tendency to focus exclusively on one's own point of view and ignore or disregard others' perspectives.

Which of the following best describes the concept of assimilation in cognitive development?

A) The process of incorporating new information into existing schemas

B) The process of modifying existing schemas to accommodate new information

C) The process of forming new schemas in response to novel experiences

D) The process of unlearning previously acquired knowledge

Correct Answer: A) The process of incorporating new information into existing schemas

Explanation: Assimilation involves incorporating new information into existing schemas or mental frameworks.

Which of the following is a characteristic of the formal operational stage of cognitive development according to Piaget?

A) Concrete operational thinking
B) Abstract and logical reasoning
C) Egocentrism
D) Lack of conservation

Correct Answer: B) Abstract and logical reasoning

Explanation: The formal operational stage, occurring from adolescence to adulthood, is

characterized by abstract and logical reasoning abilities.

Which of the following best describes the concept of zone of proximal development (ZPD) according to Lev Vygotsky?

A) The level of difficulty of tasks that a student can perform independently

B) The range of tasks that are too easy or too difficult for a student to complete

C) The difference between what a student can do independently and what they can do with assistance

D) The rate at which a student progresses through learning tasks

Correct Answer: C) The difference between what a student can do independently and what they can do with assistance

Explanation: The ZPD refers to the difference between what a student can do independently and what they can do with the assistance of a more knowledgeable other.

What is the term for the process of building on students' existing knowledge and experiences to facilitate learning?

A) Scaffolding

B) Differentiation

C) Accommodation

D) Assimilation

Correct Answer: A) Scaffolding

Explanation: Scaffolding involves providing support and guidance to learners as they work

on tasks, gradually reducing assistance as they develop competence.*

Which of the following is a characteristic of the adolescent brain?

A) Fully developed prefrontal cortex
B) Heightened risk-taking behavior
C) Stable neural connections
D) Decreased sensitivity to peer influence

Correct Answer: B) Heightened risk-taking behavior

Explanation: Adolescents often engage in heightened risk-taking behavior due to ongoing brain development and increased sensitivity to rewards.

According to Maslow's hierarchy of needs, which needs must be met before individuals can strive for self-actualization?

A) Physiological needs
B) Safety needs
C) Esteem needs
D) Belongingness and love needs

Correct Answer: A) Physiological needs

Explanation: According to Maslow, physiological needs such as food, water, and shelter must be met before individuals can strive for higher-level needs such as belongingness, esteem, and self-actualization.

Domain 3: Instructional Delivery & Facilitation

What is the primary purpose of the flipped classroom model?

A) To eliminate direct instruction from the classroom entirely

B) To shift traditional instruction outside the classroom through video lectures and use class time for hands-on activities and discussions

C) To increase the amount of teacher-led instruction in the classroom

D) To reduce student engagement in the learning process

Correct Answer: B) To shift traditional instruction outside the classroom through video lectures and use class time for hands-on activities and discussions

Explanation: In a flipped classroom model, students learn new content outside of class through video lectures or online resources, allowing for more interactive and collaborative activities during class time.

Which instructional strategy involves using real-world scenarios or problems to engage students in meaningful learning experiences?

A) Project-based learning
B) Drill and practice
C) Recitation
D) Lecture

Correct Answer: A) Project-based learning

Explanation: Project-based learning engages students in authentic, real-world projects or problems, promoting critical thinking, collaboration, and problem-solving skills.

What is the purpose of graphic organizers in the classroom?

A) To provide visual representations of information and facilitate comprehension

B) To replace traditional textbooks and written materials

C) To limit student creativity and expression

D) To assess students' understanding of concepts

Correct Answer: A) To provide visual representations of information and facilitate comprehension

Explanation: Graphic organizers visually organize information, making complex concepts more accessible and facilitating comprehension and retention of information.

Which instructional strategy involves breaking down a complex skill or task into smaller, sequential steps and teaching each step individually before combining them?

A) Direct instruction

B) Differentiated instruction

C) Backward design

D) Task analysis

Correct Answer: D) Task analysis

Explanation: Task analysis involves breaking down a complex skill or task into smaller, sequential steps, teaching each step individually, and gradually combining them to build mastery.

What is the purpose of formative feedback in the learning process?

A) To evaluate student performance at the end of a unit or course

B) To provide ongoing feedback to students to guide learning and improvement

C) To rank students based on their performance
D) To assign grades to students' work

Correct Answer: B) To provide ongoing feedback to students to guide learning and improvement

Explanation: Formative feedback is provided during the learning process to inform students about their progress, identify areas for improvement, and guide their learning journey.

Which instructional strategy involves providing students with choices in how they demonstrate their understanding of a concept or topic?

A) Direct instruction
B) Inquiry-based learning
C) Choice boards
D) Lecture

Correct Answer: C) Choice boards

Explanation: Choice boards offer students a variety of options for demonstrating their understanding of concepts or topics, promoting student autonomy and engagement in the learning process.

What is the purpose of wait time in the classroom?

A) To minimize student participation
B) To allow students time to process questions and formulate responses
C) To rush through lesson content
D) To limit student thinking and reflection

Correct Answer: B) To allow students time to process questions and formulate responses

Explanation: Wait time refers to the period of silence after a question is posed, allowing

students time to process the question, formulate responses, and engage in deeper thinking.

Which instructional strategy involves providing students with opportunities to apply their learning to real-world situations or contexts?

A) Experiential learning
B) Lecture
C) Recitation
D) Drill and practice

Correct Answer: A) Experiential learning

Explanation: Experiential learning involves learning through direct experiences, allowing students to apply their learning to real-world situations or contexts, promoting deeper understanding and skill development.

What is the purpose of peer feedback in the classroom?

A) To replace teacher feedback entirely
B) To provide students with validation of their work
C) To allow students to critique and learn from each other's work
D) To compare students' performance to one another

Correct Answer: C) To allow students to critique and learn from each other's work

Explanation: Peer feedback involves students providing constructive criticism and suggestions for improvement on each other's work, promoting collaboration, communication, and learning from peers.

Which instructional strategy involves providing students with opportunities to explore and investigate topics of interest through hands-on activities and inquiry?

A) Lecture

B) Experiential learning
C) Recitation
D) Drill and practice

Correct Answer: B) Experiential learning

Explanation: Experiential learning engages students in hands-on activities and inquiry-based exploration of topics, promoting active engagement, critical thinking, and deeper understanding.

Domain 4: Assessment Strategies

What is the primary purpose of using a variety of assessment methods in the classroom?

A) To increase students' workload
B) To provide multiple opportunities for students to demonstrate their understanding
C) To confuse students with different assessment formats
D) To simplify the grading process for teachers

Correct Answer: B) To provide multiple opportunities for students to demonstrate their understanding

Explanation: Using a variety of assessment methods allows students to demonstrate their understanding in different ways, catering to diverse learning preferences and strengths.

Which type of assessment is typically conducted during instruction to check for understanding and provide immediate feedback to students?

A) Formative assessment
B) Summative assessment
C) Diagnostic assessment
D) Authentic assessment

Correct Answer: A) Formative assessment

Explanation: Formative assessment is conducted during instruction to monitor student progress and provide immediate feedback to guide learning.

Which assessment technique involves students responding to a prompt or question orally, rather than in writing?

A) Oral assessment
B) Performance assessment
C) Portfolio assessment
D) Rubric assessment

Correct Answer: A) Oral assessment

Explanation: Oral assessment involves students responding to prompts or questions verbally, providing an opportunity to assess communication skills and understanding.

What is the primary purpose of peer review in the assessment process?

A) To assign grades to students' work
B) To provide opportunities for students to give and receive feedback on their peers' work
C) To minimize students' involvement in the assessment process
D) To evaluate students' mastery of content at the end of instruction

Correct Answer: B) To provide opportunities for students to give and receive feedback on their peers' work

Explanation: Peer review involves students providing feedback on their peers' work,

promoting collaboration, peer learning, and reflection.

Which type of assessment is typically conducted at the end of instruction to evaluate students' overall mastery of content and learning objectives?

A) Formative assessment
B) Summative assessment
C) Diagnostic assessment
D) Authentic assessment

Correct Answer: B) Summative assessment

Explanation: *Summative assessment is conducted at the end of instruction to evaluate students' overall mastery of content and learning objectives.*

What is the primary purpose of a diagnostic assessment?

A) To evaluate students' overall achievement at the end of a unit or course
B) To measure students' memorization of facts and information
C) To assign grades to students' work
D) To gauge students' prior knowledge, skills, and understanding before instruction begins

Correct Answer: D) *To gauge students' prior knowledge, skills, and understanding before instruction begins*

Explanation: *Diagnostic assessments are used to diagnose students' strengths, weaknesses, and prior knowledge before instruction begins.*

Which assessment technique involves students

completing a series of tasks or problems under standardized conditions?

A) Performance assessment
B) Portfolio assessment
C) Essay assessment
D) Standardized assessment

Correct Answer: D) Standardized assessment

Explanation: Standardized assessments involve students completing tasks or problems under standardized conditions, allowing for comparisons across students or populations.

What is the primary purpose of a checklist in assessment?

A) To measure students' memorization of facts and information
B) To track students' completion of specific tasks or criteria
C) To assign grades to students' work
D) To assess students' overall achievement at the end of a unit or course

Correct Answer: B) To track students' completion of specific tasks or criteria

Explanation: Checklists are used to track students' completion of specific tasks or criteria and provide a simple way to record whether students have met predetermined criteria.

Which assessment technique involves students selecting their best work to showcase their learning and achievement?

A) Performance assessment
B) Portfolio assessment
C) Essay assessment

D) Rubric assessment

Correct Answer: B) Portfolio assessment

Explanation: Portfolio assessment involves students selecting their best work to showcase their learning and achievement over time.

What is the primary purpose of self-assessment in the learning process?

A) To assign grades to students' work

B) To provide opportunities for students to reflect on their own learning and progress

C) To minimize students' involvement in the assessment process

D) To evaluate students' mastery of content at the end of instruction

Correct Answer: B) To provide opportunities for students to reflect on their own learning and progress

Explanation: Self-assessment involves students reflecting on their own learning experiences, accomplishments, and challenges, promoting self-awareness and metacognition.

Domain 5: Professional Development & Ethical Practice

Why is it essential for educators to engage in reflective practice?

A) To avoid accountability for their actions

B) To criticize and blame others for shortcomings

C) To continuously improve teaching effectiveness and student outcomes

D) To maintain the status quo and resist change

Answer: C) To continuously improve teaching effectiveness and student outcomes

***Explanation:** Reflective practice allows educators to critically analyze their teaching methods and strategies, identify areas for improvement, and enhance teaching effectiveness, ultimately leading to better student outcomes.*

How can educators promote diversity and inclusion in the classroom?

A) By favoring certain student groups over others

B) By ignoring the unique needs and backgrounds of students

C) By fostering a culture of respect, acceptance, and inclusivity

D) By discouraging collaboration and cooperation among students

Answer: C) By fostering a culture of respect, acceptance, and inclusivity

***Explanation:** Educators can promote diversity and inclusion by creating a classroom environment that values and respects the diverse backgrounds, experiences, and perspectives of all students.*

What role does professional ethics play in the teaching profession?

A) To promote unethical behavior and practices

B) To prioritize educators' interests over those of students

C) To guide educators' conduct and decision-making in their professional practice

D) To restrict educators' freedom of expression

Answer: C) To guide educators' conduct and decision-making in their professional practice

Explanation: Professional ethics provide educators with guidelines and principles to uphold integrity, honesty, and professionalism in their professional practice, guiding their conduct and decision-making.

Why is it important for educators to stay updated with current research and best practices in education?

A) To maintain outdated teaching methods and strategies

B) To limit students' access to quality education

C) To enhance teaching effectiveness and student learning outcomes

D) To prioritize personal interests over those of students

Answer: C) To enhance teaching effectiveness and student learning outcomes

Explanation: Staying updated with current research and best practices allows educators to incorporate evidence-based strategies and methodologies into their teaching, ultimately improving teaching effectiveness and student learning outcomes.

Which of the following is an example of an ethical dilemma commonly faced by educators?

A) Falsifying student attendance records to meet administrative requirements

B) Ignoring student safety concerns and hazards in the classroom

C) Providing preferential treatment to certain students based on personal biases

D) Respecting student privacy rights and confidentiality

Answer: C) Providing preferential treatment to certain students based on personal biases

Explanation: Providing preferential treatment based on personal biases presents an ethical dilemma for educators as it goes against principles of fairness, equity, and professionalism.

How can educators demonstrate their commitment to lifelong learning and professional growth?

A) By resisting change and innovation in teaching practices

B) By attending workshops, conferences, and professional development sessions

C) By avoiding collaboration and cooperation with colleagues

D) By isolating themselves from new research and best practices in education

Answer: B) By attending workshops, conferences, and professional development sessions

Explanation: Educators demonstrate their commitment to lifelong learning and professional growth by actively seeking opportunities for professional development, such as attending workshops, conferences, and professional development sessions.

What is the significance of maintaining confidentiality in educator-student interactions?

A) To promote transparency and accountability

B) To protect student privacy rights and confidentiality

C) To restrict student access to educational resources

D) To prioritize educators' interests over those of students

Answer: B) To protect student privacy rights and confidentiality

Explanation: Maintaining confidentiality in educator-student interactions is essential to protect student privacy rights and confidentiality, fostering trust and respect in the educator-student relationship.

Why is it important for educators to advocate for equitable access to education?

A) To perpetuate inequality and discrimination

B) To maintain the status quo and uphold existing power structures

C) To ensure that all students have equal opportunities for success

D) To prioritize the needs of privileged students over marginalized groups

Answer: C) To ensure that all students have equal opportunities for success

Explanation: Advocating for equitable access to education is essential to ensure that all students, regardless of their background or circumstances, have equal opportunities for success and fulfillment.

How can educators foster a culture of professionalism in the teaching profession?

A) By engaging in unethical behavior and practices

B) By prioritizing personal interests over those of students

C) By upholding integrity, honesty, and professionalism in their professional practice

D) By ignoring legal and ethical responsibilities

Answer: C) By upholding integrity, honesty,

and professionalism in their professional practice

***Explanation:** Educators foster a culture of professionalism by upholding integrity, honesty, and professionalism in their professional practice, setting high standards for themselves and their colleagues.*

What is the significance of collaboration between educators and community stakeholders?

A) To limit parental involvement in the education process

B) To foster a sense of exclusivity within the school community

C) To promote partnership and shared responsibility for student success

D) To prioritize educators' interests over those of students

***Answer:** C) To promote partnership and shared responsibility for student success*

***Explanation:** Collaboration between educators and community stakeholders promotes partnership and shared responsibility for student success, allowing stakeholders to work together towards common goals and objectives.*

Chapter 7
Pactice Test 4

Domain 1: Foundational Knowledge
Which of the following learning theories emphasizes the role of intrinsic motivation and self-directed learning?
A) Behaviorism
B) Cognitivism
C) Constructivism
D) Humanism
Correct Answer: D) Humanism
***Explanation:** Humanism emphasizes intrinsic motivation, self-directed learning, and the importance of personal growth and fulfillment.*

According to Piaget's theory of cognitive development, which stage is characterized by the ability to think abstractly and logically?
A) Sensorimotor
B) Preoperational
C) Concrete operational

D) Formal operational

Correct Answer: D) Formal operational

Explanation: The formal operational stage, occurring from adolescence to adulthood, is characterized by the ability to think abstractly and logically.

Which of the following best describes the concept of schema in cognitive development?

A) Inborn, biologically determined patterns of behavior

B) Mental frameworks for organizing and interpreting information

C) Learned associations between stimuli and responses

D) Units of hereditary information transmitted from parents to offspring

Correct Answer: B) Mental frameworks for organizing and interpreting information

Explanation: Schemas are mental frameworks or structures that organize and interpret information in the environment.

What is the primary purpose of summative assessment?

A) To monitor student progress and provide ongoing feedback

B) To diagnose students' strengths and weaknesses prior to instruction

C) To evaluate student achievement at the end of a unit or course

D) To promote student engagement and motivation

Correct Answer: C) To evaluate student achievement at the end of a unit or course

Explanation: Summative assessments are used to evaluate student learning outcomes at

the end of a unit, course, or instructional period.

Which of the following best describes the concept of assimilation in cognitive development?

A) The process of incorporating new information into existing schemas

B) The process of modifying existing schemas to accommodate new information

C) The process of forming new schemas in response to novel experiences

D) The process of unlearning previously acquired knowledge

Correct Answer: A) The process of incorporating new information into existing schemas

Explanation: Assimilation involves incorporating new information into existing schemas or mental frameworks.

Which ethical principle emphasizes the importance of confidentiality and trust in professional relationships?

A) Autonomy

B) Nonmaleficence

C) Veracity

D) Confidentiality

Correct Answer: D) Confidentiality

Explanation: Confidentiality is an ethical principle that emphasizes the importance of privacy, trust, and confidentiality in professional relationships.

Which of the following is a proactive classroom management strategy?

A) Reacting to misbehavior after it occurs

B) Establishing clear expectations and rules

C) Ignoring disruptive behavior
D) Punishing students for mistakes

Correct Answer: B) Establishing clear expectations and rules

Explanation: Proactive classroom management involves establishing clear expectations, rules, and routines to prevent misbehavior before it occurs.

What is the term for providing students with choices and opportunities for autonomy in learning tasks?
A) Differentiation
B) Personalization
C) Individualization
D) Autonomy

Correct Answer: D) Autonomy

Explanation: Autonomy refers to providing students with choices and opportunities for self-direction in learning tasks.

Which of the following is an example of an authentic assessment?
A) Multiple-choice test
B) Standardized test
C) Portfolio assessment
D) True-false test

Correct Answer: C) Portfolio assessment

Explanation: Portfolio assessment involves the collection and evaluation of student work samples over time to demonstrate learning and growth.

Which federal law mandates equal access to education for students with disabilities?
A) No Child Left Behind Act (NCLB)

B) Individuals with Disabilities Education Act (IDEA)

C) Every Student Succeeds Act (ESSA)

D) Americans with Disabilities Act (ADA)

Correct Answer: B) Individuals with Disabilities Education Act (IDEA)

Explanation: IDEA mandates that students with disabilities receive a free and appropriate public education (FAPE) tailored to their individual needs.

Domain 2: Student Development and Learning

Which of the following best describes the concept of nature versus nurture in human development?

A) The relative contributions of genetics and environment to human behavior and development

B) The role of heredity in shaping individual differences in behavior and personality

C) The influence of peers and social interactions on human development

D) The impact of culture on cognitive development and learning

Correct Answer: A) The relative contributions of genetics and environment to human behavior and development

Explanation: Nature versus nurture refers to the debate over the relative contributions of genetics (nature) and environment (nurture) to human behavior and development.

According to Erik Erikson's theory of psychosocial development, which stage occurs during infancy and is characterized by the development of trust and mistrust?

A) Autonomy vs. shame and doubt

B) Trust vs. mistrust

C) Initiative vs. guilt

D) Industry vs. inferiority

Correct Answer: B) Trust vs. mistrust

Explanation: The stage of trust vs. mistrust occurs during infancy and is characterized by the development of trust in caregivers.

Which of the following best describes the concept of conservation in Piaget's theory of cognitive development?

A) The ability to understand that changes in appearance do not change the quantity of an object

B) The understanding that objects continue to exist even when they are not visible

C) The ability to understand the perspectives of others and take them into account

D) The understanding that certain characteristics of objects remain the same despite changes in appearance

Correct Answer: D) The understanding that certain characteristics of objects remain the same despite changes in appearance

Explanation: Conservation refers to the understanding that certain characteristics of objects, such as quantity, volume, and mass, remain the same despite changes in appearance.

Which of the following best describes the concept of egocentrism in Piaget's theory of cognitive development?

A) The ability to understand the perspectives of others

B) The tendency to focus exclusively on one's own point of view and ignore others' perspectives

C) The understanding that objects continue to exist even when they are not visible

D) The ability to understand that changes in appearance do not change the quantity of an object

Correct Answer: B) The tendency to focus exclusively on one's own point of view and ignore others' perspectives

Explanation: Egocentrism is the tendency to focus exclusively on one's own point of view and ignore or disregard others' perspectives.

Which of the following best describes the concept of assimilation in cognitive development?

A) The process of incorporating new information into existing schemas

B) The process of modifying existing schemas to accommodate new information

C) The process of forming new schemas in response to novel experiences

D) The process of unlearning previously acquired knowledge

Correct Answer: A) The process of incorporating new information into existing schemas

Explanation: Assimilation involves incorporating new information into existing schemas or mental frameworks.

Which of the following is a characteristic of the formal operational stage of cognitive development according to Piaget?

A) Concrete operational thinking
B) Abstract and logical reasoning
C) Egocentrism
D) Lack of conservation

Correct Answer: B) Abstract and logical reasoning

Explanation: The formal operational stage, occurring from adolescence to adulthood, is characterized by abstract and logical reasoning abilities.

Which of the following best describes the concept of zone of proximal development (ZPD) according to Lev Vygotsky?

A) The level of difficulty of tasks that a student can perform independently

B) The range of tasks that are too easy or too difficult for a student to complete

C) The difference between what a student can do independently and what they can do with assistance

D) The rate at which a student progresses through learning tasks

Correct Answer: C) The difference between what a student can do independently and what they can do with assistance

Explanation: The ZPD refers to the difference between what a student can do independently and what they can do with the assistance of a more knowledgeable other.

What is the term for the process of building on students' existing knowledge and experiences to facilitate learning?

A) Scaffolding
B) Differentiation
C) Accommodation
D) Assimilation

Correct Answer: A) Scaffolding

Explanation: Scaffolding involves providing support and guidance to learners as they work

on tasks, gradually reducing assistance as they develop competence.*

Which of the following is a characteristic of the adolescent brain?
A) Fully developed prefrontal cortex
B) Heightened risk-taking behavior
C) Stable neural connections
D) Decreased sensitivity to peer influence

Correct Answer: B) Heightened risk-taking behavior

Explanation: Adolescents often engage in heightened risk-taking behavior due to ongoing brain development and increased sensitivity to rewards.

According to Maslow's hierarchy of needs, which needs must be met before individuals can strive for self-actualization?
A) Physiological needs
B) Safety needs
C) Esteem needs
D) Belongingness and love needs

Correct Answer: A) Physiological needs

Explanation: According to Maslow, physiological needs such as food, water, and shelter must be met before individuals can strive for higher-level needs such as belongingness, esteem, and self-actualization.

Domain 3: Instructional Delivery & Facilitation

Which instructional strategy focuses on breaking down complex tasks into smaller, more manageable steps to facilitate learning?

A) Direct instruction
B) Differentiated instruction
C) Scaffolded instruction
D) Collaborative learning

Correct Answer: C) Scaffolded instruction

Explanation: Scaffolded instruction involves providing support and guidance to students as they work on tasks, gradually reducing assistance as they develop competence.

What is the primary goal of cooperative learning activities in the classroom?

A) To promote competition among students
B) To encourage individual achievement only
C) To foster collaboration and teamwork among students
D) To minimize student interaction during lessons

Correct Answer: C) To foster collaboration and teamwork among students

Explanation: Cooperative learning activities aim to promote collaboration, teamwork, and peer interaction to enhance learning outcomes.

Which technology tool allows educators to create interactive multimedia presentations for instructional purposes?

A) Spreadsheet software
B) Presentation software
C) Word processing software
D) Database software

Correct Answer: B) Presentation software

Explanation: Presentation software, such as PowerPoint or Google Slides, allows educators to create interactive multimedia presentations to deliver instructional content.

In the context of classroom assessment, what is the purpose of formative assessment?

A) To evaluate student learning at the end of a unit or course

B) To provide feedback to students during the learning process

C) To rank students based on their performance

D) To assign grades to students' work

Correct Answer: B) To provide feedback to students during the learning process

Explanation: Formative assessment is used to provide ongoing feedback to students to inform instruction and support learning during the learning process.

Which teaching method involves presenting information in a step-by-step sequence, providing clear explanations and examples along the way?

A) Inquiry-based learning

B) Direct instruction

C) Problem-based learning

D) Experiential learning

Correct Answer: B) Direct instruction

Explanation: Direct instruction involves presenting information in a structured, step-by-step manner, providing clear explanations and examples to facilitate learning.

What is the purpose of a KWL chart in the classroom?

A) To summarize key concepts learned during a lesson

B) To assess students' prior knowledge before a lesson

C) To organize information about a topic before, during, and after learning

D) To track students' progress on learning objectives

Correct Answer: C) To organize information about a topic before, during, and after learning

Explanation: A KWL chart is a graphic organizer used to activate prior knowledge, set learning goals, and organize new information before, during, and after learning.

Which instructional strategy involves presenting students with open-ended questions or problems to solve, encouraging critical thinking and problem-solving skills?

A) Drill and practice
B) Socratic questioning
C) Lecture
D) Recitation

Correct Answer: B) Socratic questioning

Explanation: Socratic questioning involves posing open-ended questions or problems to students to stimulate critical thinking, discussion, and deeper understanding of concepts.

What is the primary purpose of a think-aloud strategy in the classroom?

A) To encourage students to think silently about a concept
B) To help students develop metacognitive awareness by verbalizing their thought processes
C) To provide direct instruction on a topic
D) To assess students' understanding of a concept

Correct Answer: B) To help students develop metacognitive awareness by verbalizing their thought processes

Explanation: The think-aloud strategy involves students verbalizing their thought processes while solving problems or completing tasks, helping them develop metacognitive awareness and self-monitoring skills.

Which technology tool allows educators to create interactive quizzes and assessments for students?

A) Learning management system (LMS)
B) Video conferencing software
C) Assessment authoring tool
D) Social media platform

Correct Answer: C) Assessment authoring tool

Explanation: Assessment authoring tools allow educators to create interactive quizzes and assessments with various question types, such as multiple-choice, short answer, and matching, to assess student learning.

What is the primary purpose of differentiated instruction in the classroom?

A) To provide students with the same instructional materials and activities
B) To tailor instruction to meet the diverse needs of individual students
C) To focus solely on students' academic strengths
D) To minimize student engagement in the learning process

Correct Answer: B) To tailor instruction to meet the diverse needs of individual students

Explanation: Differentiated instruction involves adjusting instructional content, process, and product to accommodate the diverse learning needs, interests, and readiness levels of individual students.

Domain 4: Assessment Strategies

Which of the following is an example of an authentic assessment task?

A) Multiple-choice quiz
B) Essay exam
C) Real-world project
D) Vocabulary test

Correct Answer: C) Real-world project

Explanation: Authentic assessment tasks mirror real-world challenges or scenarios, such as completing a project that simulates tasks professionals might encounter in their field.

What is the primary purpose of using a rubric in assessment?

A) To assign grades based on subjective judgment
B) To provide students with feedback on their performance
C) To ensure consistency and fairness in grading
D) To eliminate the need for qualitative assessment

Correct Answer: C) To ensure consistency and fairness in grading

Explanation: Rubrics outline specific criteria for assessment, providing clear expectations and ensuring consistency in grading across different students or evaluators.

Which assessment method is best suited for assessing students' ability to perform a specific task or demonstrate a skill?

A) Multiple-choice test
B) Performance assessment
C) Essay exam
D) Portfolio assessment

Correct Answer: B) Performance assessment

Explanation: Performance assessment tasks require students to demonstrate their abilities in real-world tasks or scenarios, making them ideal for assessing skills and abilities.

In assessment, what does the term "validity" refer to?

A) Consistency of measurement

B) Accuracy of measurement

C) Extent to which a test measures what it is intended to measure

D) Extent to which a test produces similar results on different occasions

Correct Answer: C) Extent to which a test measures what it is intended to measure

Explanation: Validity refers to the degree to which a test accurately measures the knowledge, skills, or attributes it is intended to measure.

Which type of assessment is most appropriate for diagnosing students' learning needs and prior knowledge?

A) Summative assessment

B) Formative assessment

C) Diagnostic assessment

D) Authentic assessment

Correct Answer: C) Diagnostic assessment

Explanation: Diagnostic assessments are designed to identify students' strengths, weaknesses, and prior knowledge before instruction begins, making them ideal for diagnosing learning needs.

What is the primary purpose of using portfolios in assessment?

A) To assign grades based on students' overall performance

B) To provide a record of students' work over time
C) To eliminate the need for traditional assessments
D) To simplify the grading process for teachers

Correct Answer: B) To provide a record of students' work over time

Explanation: Portfolios compile samples of students' work over time, providing a comprehensive record of their learning and progress.

Which assessment technique involves students reflecting on their learning experiences and setting goals for improvement?
A) Self-assessment
B) Peer assessment
C) Performance assessment
D) Rubric assessment

Correct Answer: A) Self-assessment

Explanation: Self-assessment involves students reflecting on their own learning experiences, strengths, weaknesses, and setting goals for improvement.

What is the primary purpose of using peer assessment in the classroom?
A) To assign grades based on students' evaluations of their peers' work
B) To provide opportunities for students to give and receive feedback on their peers' work
C) To minimize teachers' involvement in the assessment process
D) To eliminate the need for traditional assessments

Correct Answer: B) To provide opportunities for students to give and receive feedback on their peers' work

Explanation: Peer assessment involves students providing feedback on their peers' work, promoting collaboration, peer learning, and reflection.

Which type of assessment is typically conducted at the end of instruction to evaluate students' overall mastery of content?

A) Formative assessment
B) Summative assessment
C) Diagnostic assessment
D) Authentic assessment

Correct Answer: B) Summative assessment

Explanation: Summative assessments are conducted at the end of instruction to evaluate students' overall mastery of content and learning objectives.

What is the primary purpose of using authentic assessment in the classroom?

A) To measure students' memorization of facts and information
B) To provide opportunities for students to apply their learning in real-world contexts
C) To assign grades based on subjective judgment
D) To eliminate the need for traditional assessments

Correct Answer: B) To provide opportunities for students to apply their learning in real-world contexts

Explanation: Authentic assessment tasks mirror real-world challenges or scenarios, allowing students to apply their learning in authentic contexts.

. . .

Domain 5: Professional Development & Ethical Practice

What is the primary purpose of engaging in continuing professional development as an educator?

A) To fulfill mandatory training requirements
B) To earn higher salaries and bonuses
C) To enhance teaching skills and knowledge
D) To decrease workload and stress levels

Correct Answer: C) To enhance teaching skills and knowledge

Explanation: Continuing professional development allows educators to stay updated with the latest research, methodologies, and best practices in teaching, ultimately improving their effectiveness in the classroom.

Which of the following is an example of a professional code of conduct for educators?

A) The Hippocratic Oath
B) The Nuremberg Code
C) The National Education Association Code of Ethics
D) The Magna Carta

Correct Answer: C) The National Education Association Code of Ethics

Explanation: The National Education Association (NEA) Code of Ethics outlines the ethical principles and standards of professional conduct for educators in the United States.

What is the purpose of legal requirements for educators in the teaching profession?

A) To restrict educators' freedom of expression
B) To ensure compliance with state and federal laws
C) To promote inequality and discrimination

D) To discourage educators from seeking professional development

Correct Answer: B) To ensure compliance with state and federal laws

Explanation: Legal requirements for educators are designed to ensure that educators adhere to laws and regulations governing education, safeguarding the rights and well-being of students.

Which of the following is an ethical dilemma commonly faced by educators?

A) Choosing a favorite student to receive special treatment

B) Falsifying student test scores to meet performance targets

C) Encouraging students to cheat on exams

D) Allowing bullying behavior to go unaddressed in the classroom

Correct Answer: D) Allowing bullying behavior to go unaddressed in the classroom

Explanation: Allowing bullying behavior to go unaddressed presents an ethical dilemma for educators, as they must balance their duty to maintain a safe and inclusive learning environment with concerns about student privacy and confidentiality.

Which of the following is a key aspect of collaborative relationships with colleagues and the community?

A) Isolating oneself from other educators

B) Resisting opportunities for professional growth and development

C) Engaging in teamwork and cooperation

D) Ignoring input from parents and community stakeholders

Correct Answer: C) Engaging in teamwork and cooperation

Explanation: Collaborative relationships with colleagues and the community involve working together, sharing ideas, resources, and expertise to support student success and school improvement efforts.

What is the role of educators in promoting social justice and equity in education?

A) To perpetuate inequality and discrimination

B) To maintain the status quo and uphold existing power structures

C) To advocate for fairness, inclusivity, and equal opportunities for all students

D) To prioritize the needs of privileged students over marginalized groups

Correct Answer: C) To advocate for fairness, inclusivity, and equal opportunities for all students

Explanation: Educators play a critical role in promoting social justice and equity in education by advocating for fairness, inclusivity, and equal opportunities for all students, regardless of background or circumstances.

Which of the following is an example of a collaborative relationship with colleagues?

A) Competing with colleagues for recognition and rewards

B) Sharing teaching strategies and resources with colleagues

C) Ignoring colleagues' input and feedback

D) Refusing to collaborate on team projects or initiatives

Correct Answer: B) Sharing teaching strategies and resources with colleagues

Explanation: Collaborative relationships with colleagues involve sharing ideas, resources, and best practices to support each other's professional growth and improve student outcomes.

What is the purpose of establishing collaborative relationships with parents and community stakeholders?

A) To limit parental involvement in the education process

B) To create a sense of exclusivity and elitism within the school community

C) To foster a sense of partnership and shared responsibility for student success

D) To maintain a barrier between the school and the surrounding community

Correct Answer: C) To foster a sense of partnership and shared responsibility for student success

Explanation: Collaborative relationships with parents and community stakeholders involve working together to support student learning and well-being, fostering a sense of partnership and shared responsibility.

Which of the following is an example of a legal requirement for educators?

A) Encouraging students to engage in risky behaviors

B) Violating students' privacy rights by sharing confidential information

C) Providing a safe and inclusive learning environment for all students

D) Fostering a supportive and nurturing classroom climate

Correct Answer: B) Violating students' privacy rights by sharing confidential information

Explanation: Educators are legally obligated to protect students' privacy rights by safeguarding confidential information and only sharing it when necessary and appropriate.

How does engaging in collaborative relationships with colleagues and community stakeholders benefit educators and students?

A) It increases competition and rivalry among educators

B) It fosters a sense of teamwork and cooperation

C) It limits opportunities for professional growth and development

D) It excludes parents and community members from the education process

Correct Answer: B) It fosters a sense of teamwork and cooperation

Explanation: Collaborative relationships with colleagues and community stakeholders promote teamwork, cooperation, and shared responsibility for student success, ultimately benefiting educators and students alike.

Chapter 8
Additional Resources

Below, you will find some additional resources to help you prepare for your FTCE Professional Education Test.

Official FTCE Professional Education Test Study Guide

This guide, provided by the Florida Department of Education, offers an overview of the test format, sample questions, and preparation strategies.

FTCE Professional Education Test Prep Books

There are several books available specifically designed to help candidates prepare for the FTCE Professional Education Test. Look for comprehensive guides that cover all test domains and include practice questions and explanations.

Online Practice Tests

Many websites offer online practice tests for the FTCE Professional Education Test. These tests can help you familiarize yourself with the format and content of the exam and identify areas where you may need additional study.

There are several websites where you can find FTCE Professional Education Test prep help. Here are some options:

- ***Florida Department of Education Website***: The official website of the Florida Department of Education often provides resources, study guides, and practice tests specifically for the FTCE Professional Education Test.
- ***Mometrix Test Preparation***: Mometrix offers a range of study materials for the FTCE Professional Education Test, including study guides, flashcards, and practice tests.
- ***Teachers Test Prep***: Teachers Test Prep provides online courses, study guides, and practice tests for various teacher certification exams, including the FTCE Professional Education Test.
- ***Study.com***: Study.com offers comprehensive study guides, practice tests, and video lessons covering topics relevant to the FTCE Professional Education Test.
- ***PraxisPrep.com***: While primarily focused on Praxis exams, PraxisPrep.com also offers resources and practice tests for other teacher

certification exams, including the FTCE Professional Education Test.
- **Kaplan Test Prep**: Kaplan offers test prep courses, study guides, and practice tests for a wide range of exams, including the FTCE Professional Education Test.
- **Test Prep Toolkit**: Test Prep Toolkit provides free practice questions and study guides for various standardized tests, including the FTCE Professional Education Test.
- **Teachers Test Review**: Teachers Test Review offers study guides, flashcards, and practice tests for teacher certification exams, including the FTCE Professional Education Test.
- **Magoosh**: Magoosh offers online test prep courses and study materials for a variety of exams, including teacher certification tests like the FTCE Professional Education Test.
- **YouTube**: You can also find instructional videos, tutorials, and tips for FTCE Professional Education Test prep on YouTube. Many educators and test prep companies share helpful content for free.

Before purchasing any study materials or courses, be sure to research reviews and consider your own learning preferences to find the best fit for your needs.

FTCE Professional Education Test Prep Courses

Consider enrolling in an online or in-person prep course specifically tailored to the FTCE Professional Education Test. These courses often include expert instruction, study materials, and practice exams.

Educational Psychology Textbooks

Since the FTCE Professional Education Test covers topics such as educational psychology, instructional design, and assessment principles, textbooks in these areas can be valuable resources for deeper understanding of key concepts.

Teacher Certification Forums and Communities

Joining online forums and communities dedicated to teacher certification exams can provide valuable insights and support from fellow test-takers. You can ask questions, share tips, and learn from others' experiences.

Flashcards

Using flashcards can be an effective way to review key concepts and terms covered on the FTCE Professional Education Test. You can create your own flashcards or find pre-made sets online or in study guides.

Educational Websites and Blogs

Explore educational websites and blogs that offer articles, tutorials, and resources on topics relevant to the FTCE Professional Education Test. These resources can provide additional explanations and insights to supplement your study materials.

Review Sessions and Workshops

Look for review sessions or workshops offered by educational institutions, test prep companies, or professional organizations. These sessions often provide focused review of test content and strategies for success.

Practice Teaching and Observation

If possible, engage in practice teaching opportunities or observe experienced educators in action. This hands-on experience can help reinforce your understanding of instructional practices and classroom management techniques.

Remember to utilize a variety of resources and study methods to tailor your preparation to your individual learning style and needs. Good luck with your FTCE Professional Education Test preparation!

Chapter 9
Contact Information for FTCE Support

To obtain contact information for FTCE (Florida Teacher Certification Examinations) support, you can visit the official FTCE website or contact the Florida Department of Education directly. Here's how to do it:

Official FTCE Website: Visit the official FTCE website maintained by the Florida Department of Education. You can find contact information, frequently asked questions (FAQs), and other resources related to the FTCE exams. The website URL is typically www.fl.nesinc.com.

Contact Information on the Website: Navigate to the "Contact Us" or "Support" section of the FTCE website. Here, you should find contact details such as phone numbers, email addresses, and mailing addresses for FTCE support services.

Chapter 10
Final Review and Test Preparation Plan

Final Review and Test Preparation Plan

As you approach the final stages of your preparation for the FTCE Professional Education Test, it's essential to organize your efforts efficiently and ensure that you're fully prepared for success on exam day. This chapter will guide you through creating a study schedule, provide a checklist for test day, and offer some final tips and encouragement to boost your confidence.

Creating a Study Schedule

A well-structured study schedule serves as a roadmap to guide your preparation for the FTCE Professional Education Test, ensuring that you cover all necessary material while maximizing your retention of key concepts. Here's a more detailed approach to creating your study schedule:

Assess Your Current Knowledge

Before diving into your study schedule, take some time to assess your strengths and weaknesses in each test domain. Reflect on your previous coursework, teaching experiences, and areas of expertise. Identify topics where you feel confident and those that require more attention.

This self-assessment will help you prioritize your study efforts.

Set Realistic Goals

Determine the amount of time you have available until your test date and divide your study material accordingly. Set realistic, achievable goals for each study session, whether daily or weekly, to ensure you cover all content areas adequately. Break down larger topics into smaller, manageable chunks to make your goals more attainable.

Allocate Study Time

Schedule regular study sessions throughout the week, taking into account your other commitments and responsibilities. Establish a consistent study routine and stick to it as much as possible. Be sure to include breaks for rest and relaxation to prevent burnout and maintain focus during your study sessions.

Use Variety in Study Methods

Keep your study sessions engaging and effective by incorporating a variety of study methods. Mix and match activities such as reading from textbooks or study guides, reviewing your notes and annotations, practicing with sample questions or flashcards, and engaging in discussions with peers or instructors. Experiment with different study techniques to find what works best for you.

Practice with Timed Tests

As your test date approaches, gradually introduce timed practice tests into your study schedule. Simulating the exam environment will help you become more comfortable with the format and pacing of the test while improving your time management skills. Aim to complete full-length practice tests under timed conditions to accurately gauge your readiness and identify areas for further improvement.

Review Regularly

Schedule periodic review sessions to reinforce your understanding of key concepts and ensure retention over time. Set aside dedicated time to revisit previously covered material, focusing on areas where you may need additional clarification or practice. Use review sessions to consolidate your learning and address any lingering questions or uncertainties.

Stay Flexible

Remain adaptable and be prepared to adjust your study schedule as needed based on your progress and any unexpected circumstances that may arise. Life can be unpredictable, so it's essential to build flexibility into your plan to accommodate changes in your schedule or unforeseen challenges. Stay resilient and stay committed to your goals, adjusting your study plan as necessary to stay on track toward success.

Checklist for Test Day

On the day of your FTCE Professional Education Test, being well-prepared and organized can contribute significantly to your overall performance. Use this checklist to ensure you have everything you need for a smooth and successful testing experience:

Admission Ticket

Print out your admission ticket well in advance of the test date. Double-check the details, including the test date, time, and location. Make sure you have a clear understanding of where you need to go and when you need to be there.

Valid Identification

Bring a current, government-issued photo ID with you to the testing center. Accepted forms of ID typically include a driver's license, passport, or state ID card. Ensure that your ID is not expired and that the name matches the one used during registration.

Approved Testing Aids

Review the guidelines provided by the testing authority to determine which items are allowed in the testing room. Commonly permitted items include pencils, erasers, a basic calculator (if permitted), and any other specified materials. Ensure that your testing aids comply with the rules to avoid any issues during the exam.

Snacks and Water

Pack a small snack and a bottle of water to keep you energized and hydrated during the exam. Choose snacks that are easy to eat and won't cause distractions, such as granola bars, nuts, or fruit. Staying hydrated and nourished can help maintain your focus and concentration throughout the test.

Comfortable Clothing

Dress comfortably and in layers to accommodate variations in temperature within the testing room. Opt for clothing that allows you to move freely and comfortably while sitting for an extended period. Avoid wearing anything too restrictive or uncomfortable that may distract you during the exam.

Arrival Time

Plan to arrive at the testing center well ahead of the scheduled start time. Aim to arrive at least 30 minutes early to allow ample time for parking, navigating the building, and completing check-in procedures. Arriving early can help alleviate stress and ensure that you're settled and ready to begin the exam on time.

By following this checklist and adequately preparing for

test day, you can approach the FTCE Professional Education Test with confidence and focus, giving yourself the best chance of success. Remember to stay calm, stay focused, and trust in your preparation—you've got this!

Final Tips and Encouragement

As you approach the culmination of your test preparation journey, it's natural to experience a mix of emotions, ranging from excitement to nervousness. However, with the right mindset and strategies, you can navigate this final stage with confidence and composure. Here are some additional tips and words of encouragement to support you along the way:

Trust Your Preparation

You've invested considerable time and effort into preparing for this exam, diligently studying and honing your skills. Trust in the depth of your preparation and the knowledge you've acquired throughout your journey. Have confidence in your abilities, knowing that you've equipped yourself with the necessary tools to tackle the challenges that lie ahead.

Stay Calm and Focused

On the day of the test, it's crucial to maintain a calm and focused demeanor. Take deep breaths to center yourself and alleviate any pre-exam jitters. Remind yourself that you are well-prepared and capable of handling whatever comes your way. Focus your attention fully on each question, blocking out any distractions or external pressures. By staying present and composed, you can approach each question with clarity and precision.

Read Directions Carefully

As you navigate through the exam, pay close attention to all instructions and question prompts. Take the time to read each direction thoroughly to ensure a clear understanding of what is being asked. Avoid making assumptions or rushing through the instructions, as overlooking important details could lead to unnecessary errors. By carefully following the directions, you can approach each question with confidence and accuracy.

Manage Your Time Wisely

Time management is critical during the exam, so it's essential to allocate your time wisely across all sections and questions. Pace yourself throughout the test, ensuring that you devote an appropriate amount of time to each item without lingering too long on any single question. If you encounter a challenging question, don't hesitate to mark it for review and move on to the next one. By effectively managing your time, you can maximize your chances of completing the exam successfully.

Review Your Answers

If time permits, take advantage of the opportunity to review your answers before submitting your exam. Use this time to double-check your work, looking for any errors or inconsistencies that may require correction. Pay particular attention to questions where you had uncertainties or hesitations, revisiting them with a fresh perspective. By conducting a thorough review, you can identify any areas needing clarification or revision, ensuring the highest level of accuracy in your responses.

Embrace Every Experience as a Learning Opportunity

Regardless of the outcome of the exam, view each experience as an invaluable opportunity for growth and development. Every challenge you encounter serves as a stepping stone on your journey to becoming a certified educator.

Embrace the lessons learned along the way, recognizing that each setback or success contributes to your overall growth and progress. Stay resilient in the face of adversity, remaining steadfast in your commitment to achieving your goals.

As you embark on this final leg of your journey, remember that you are capable, resilient, and well-prepared to tackle the challenges that lie ahead. Trust in your abilities, stay focused on your goals, and believe in the limitless potential that resides within you. With determination, perseverance, and a positive mindset, there's no limit to what you can accomplish. You've worked hard to reach this point—now go out there and show the world what you're capable of. Success is within your grasp—you've got this!

Chapter 11
Glossary of Key Terms

Assessment Literacy: Understanding of assessment principles, techniques, and practices, including interpretation of assessment results.

Authentic Assessment: Assessment tasks that require students to apply knowledge and skills in real-world contexts.

Behavior Management: Strategies for promoting positive behavior and addressing challenging behaviors in the classroom.

Classroom Management: Strategies and techniques used to create a positive and productive learning environment.

Collaboration: Working with colleagues to share ideas, resources, and best practices to improve teaching and learning.

Collaborative Learning: Learning that occurs through collaboration and interaction with others.

Cultural Competence: Ability to interact effectively with people from different cultural backgrounds.

Curriculum Development: Process of designing, implementing, and evaluating curriculum frameworks.

Data Analysis: Examination and interpretation of assessment data to inform instructional decision-making.

Differentiation: Adapting instruction to meet individual student needs, interests, and learning styles.

Digital Literacy: Ability to find, evaluate, and use digital information effectively and responsibly.

Diversity: Range of differences among individuals, including but not limited to culture, language, and ability.

Equity: Concept of fairness and impartiality, ensuring equal access to opportunities and resources.

Ethical Conduct: Behavior aligning with moral principles, standards, and values, especially in professional settings.

Formative Assessment: Assessment conducted during the learning process to provide feedback and guide instruction.

Inclusion: Practice of ensuring all students, regardless of background or abilities, are included in classroom activities.

Instructional Design: Planning and organization of instructional materials and activities to facilitate learning.

Learning Environment: Physical and psychological setting that influences student learning and engagement.

Lifelong Learning: Continuous pursuit of knowledge and skills throughout one's life.

Motivation: Psychological factors influencing behavior and effort towards achieving goals.

Pedagogy: Method and practice of teaching, especially as an academic subject or theoretical concept.

Professional Development: Activities designed to improve professional knowledge, skills, and effectiveness.

Professional Ethics: Moral principles and standards guiding professional behavior and conduct.

Professionalism: Conduct, behavior, and attitude characterized by competence, integrity, and ethical behavior.

Reflective Practice: Process of reflecting on experiences, actions, and beliefs to improve professional practice.

Social Justice: Pursuit of equality and fairness in society, addressing systemic inequalities.

Standardized Testing: Assessment administered and scored according to predetermined standards or criteria.

Student-Centered Learning: Instructional approach focusing on student needs, interests, and abilities.

Summative Assessment: Assessment conducted at the end of a learning period to evaluate student learning outcomes.

Teacher Collaboration: Working with colleagues to share ideas, resources, and best practices to improve teaching and learning.

Technology Integration: Incorporation of technology into teaching and learning activities.

Chapter 12
Summary of Key Theories and Models

Behaviorism

This theory posits that behavior is learned through conditioning, which involves the association of stimuli with responses. Key figures associated with behaviorism include Ivan Pavlov, John B. Watson, and B.F. Skinner.

Cognitivism

Cognitivism focuses on the mental processes involved in learning, such as perception, memory, and problem-solving. Key figures in cognitivism include Jean Piaget, Lev Vygotsky, and Jerome Bruner.

Constructivism

Constructivism emphasizes the active construction of knowledge by learners through interaction with their environment. Learners build upon prior knowledge and experiences to construct new understanding. Piaget and Vygotsky also contributed to constructivist theories.

Connectivism

Connectivism is a relatively modern theory that emphasizes the role of technology and networks in learning. It suggests that learning is distributed across networks of people, resources, and technology, and that the ability to navigate these networks is crucial for learning in the digital age.

Multiple Intelligences

Developed by Howard Gardner, the theory of multiple intelligences proposes that intelligence is not a single, fixed trait, but rather a set of distinct abilities or intelligences. These include linguistic, logical-mathematical, spatial, bodily-kinesthetic, musical, interpersonal, intrapersonal, and naturalistic intelligences.

Blooms Taxonomy

Blooms Taxonomy is a hierarchical framework for categorizing educational objectives. It consists of six levels: remembering, understanding, applying, analyzing, evaluating, and creating. It is often used to guide the design of learning activities and assessments.

Vygotsky's Zone of Proximal Development (ZPD)

Vygotsky's ZPD refers to the difference between what a learner can do independently and what they can achieve with guidance and support from a more knowledgeable individual. It highlights the importance of scaffolding and social interaction in learning.

Gardner's Theory of Multiple Intelligences

Gardner proposed that intelligence is not a single, monolithic trait, but rather a diverse set of abilities or intelligences, including linguistic, logical-mathematical, spatial, bodily-kinesthetic, musical, interpersonal, intrapersonal, and naturalistic intelligences.

These theories and models provide educators with valuable frameworks for understanding how learning occurs and how to design effective instruction that meets the diverse needs of learners. Understanding these theories is crucial for educators preparing for the FTCE Professional Education Test as they inform instructional practices and pedagogical approaches.

www.ingramcontent.com/pod-product-compliance
Lightning Source LLC
LaVergne TN
LVHW021827060526
838201LV00058B/3545